A VERY PRESENT HELP

**A Story of God's Grace
in the Midst of Tragedy**

Kathryn S. Cadarette

ACW Press
Eugene, Oregon 97405

A Very Present Help

Cover Design by Alpha Advertising
Interior Design by Pine Hill Graphics

Packaged by ACW Press
85334 Lorane Hwy
Eugene, Oregon 97405
www.acwpress.com
The views expressed or implied in this work do not necessarily reflect those of ACW
Press. Ultimate design, content, and editorial accuracy of this work is the responsibil-
ity of the author(s).

Library of Congress Cataloging-in-Publication Data
(Provided by Cassidy Cataloguing Services, Inc.)

Cadarette, Kathryn S.

   A very present help : a story of God's grace in the midst of tragedy /
Kathryn S. Cadarette. -- 1st ed. -- Eugene, Ore. : ACW Press, 2003.

    p. ; cm.

    ISBN: 1-932124-16-0

   1. Grief--Religious aspects. 2. Presence of God. 3. Church work with
the sick. 4. Church work with the bereaved. 5. Methodist Church--Clergy-
-Biography. 6. Cancer--Patients--Biography. I. Title.

BV4909 .C33 2003
259/.4--dc22   0311

Printed in the United States of America.

Dedicated:

—to the memory of a true friend.

—to the inspiration of my parents' faith.

—to the support of a loving husband.

—to the joy of serving a very present God.

Prologue

Moses has inspired a lot of envy through the years.

When I first entered seminary, I found most of us candidates for ministry were unclear about our call to ministry. While we felt we were answering God's call, we admitted that we wished we could have had a burning-bush encounter like Moses, with God's booming voice giving us specific information about our futures.

Likewise as a pastor, I found many parishioners were unclear what God was saying to them. They too would refer to Moses and wonder why in the midst of their struggles, God wouldn't speak directly to them. Because they didn't have the burning-bush encounter with God, they thought God was far away or didn't care to answer them.

For all of us, I offer this book—a reflection on five years of God's presence in our lives. For in the midst of tragedy, I learned the truth offered by the Psalmist in chapter 46, verse 1: *"God is our refuge and strength, a very present help in trouble."*

This is the story of Cathy Cadarette, a friend who faced cancer, and of her husband, Dave Cadarette, as he struggled to find answers in his sorrow. This is my story, as I ministered in my first parish—and allowed my parishioners to minister to me.

But most of all, it is God's story: of how God was present to all three of us as we doubted, feared, questioned and—yes—was even present as we celebrated. God worked in all three of our lives, affirming that God is alive and loves us.

Most of all, it demonstrates how God offers to be a very present help at every crossroad in our spiritual journeys.

Chapter

*I thank Christ Jesus our Lord, who has given
me strength, and who judged me faithful enough
to call me into his service.*
—I Timothy 1:12

It was unthinkable—a room full of ministers, yet no one took up a collection.

But this night, the pastors weren't in charge. The Gideons, a men's organization that distributes Bibles, had invited about twenty clergy from northwest Michigan to its annual pastor appreciation dinner.

Waitresses cleared the last of the dishes from our tables as we turned our chairs toward the lectern. The emcee clearly was ready to begin the program. "But before we begin," he announced cheerily, "we'd like to go around the room and have the pastors introduce themselves and introduce their wives."

In turn, each six-foot-something pastor stood. Each used his best "preacher's voice"—a voice heard not only by everyone in our room, but probably in the entire restaurant—to introduce himself and then add a few complimentary words for the woman beside him.

Then it was my turn. I rose to my five-foot-two stature—of which one inch was high heels—and began my introduction, noticing that a few people had to lean in to hear me.

"Hi. I'm Kathy Slaughter, the new pastor at Horton Bay United Methodist Church. And," I added, grinning at the emcee, "my wife couldn't be here tonight."

Now I realize some of my radical clergy sisters would have lectured the Gideons on how, this being 1994, women were not only being ordained as pastors, but as bishops. They might even have noted that the Gideons knew I was coming and should have modified their introduction.

But in my first year at Horton Bay United Methodist Church, I was anything but radical even if I was a newly-ordained clergywoman. (By the way, don't call me a "lady preacher." We don't talk about "gentlemen preachers." At the very least, it seems we should be called "female pastors," using the correct adjective describing gender.)

(OK, sometimes I do get a little radical.)

But mostly, I find humor and joy in being a person, a woman, a Christian, a pastor—just in being a child of God. And since being appointed that summer to Horton Bay, I found joy and humor helped many people accept having their first female pastor.

With just over sixty members, the church was more populous than the village of Horton Bay. I soon found my members were more likely to have bread machines than answering machines in their homes. So although it was disturbing that I couldn't leave a message to let parishioners know I had called, at least when I did get to visit their homes, I was met with homemade bread.

The congregation had its roots in the Evangelical Church, and continued to be conservative in its theology. As I came to know the members, I realized they were just as concerned as I with whether we would mesh as parish and pastor.

But as I settled into the parsonage, I nailed a plaque to the wall in my study. A present from my Uncle Frank and Aunt Juanita, the plaque contained the words of I Timothy 1:12: "I thank Christ Jesus our Lord, who has given me strength, and who judged me faithful enough to call me into His service."

I can handle "faithful enough." I would never claim to be perfect, to have all the answers, to even begin to understand why God called me from nine years as a newspaper journalist to enter into ordained ministry.

But in that verse, I am always reminded that God is my strength, and God simply seeks for me to be "faithful enough" to respond to the call to serve. God didn't choose me because I was female or good with words; God simply chose me because I was willing to say yes.

In the summer of 1994, even as I was settling into the parsonage, another family in Horton Bay was about to learn about what it meant to be "faithful enough."

Less than a mile from the church, Dave and Cathy Cadarette were raising their three children. None of the family had been inside our building to worship. Although Cathy had been active in her church as a teenager, Dave had only one experience of church people, back in their hometown of Alpena, Mich.

On their first Christmas Eve as a family, Dave and Cathy went to evening services with their infant daughter, Amy. Cathy directed Dave to the back pew because she knew the heat register was located there. On this holiest of nights, as the people reflected upon the birth of a baby who would be their Savior, Dave and Cathy's baby cooed in Cathy's arms, singing her own hymns of praise to God.

To which one church member responded by turning around and telling the young couple, "You should keep that child at home until she knows how to behave in church."

After that night, Dave refused to set foot in a church. However, he had set foot *on* Horton Bay church. In the early 1980s, he had moved his family from Alpena to Horton Bay to start a roofing business, and one of the first buildings he worked on was the church. He became acquainted with a few members of the congregation, but as soon as he was finished with the job, it was the end of his association with the church.

By 1994, Amy was ready to start her senior year at Aquinas College in Grand Rapids. Brent and David Jr. were a senior and freshman respectively at Boyne City High School, involved in almost every sport offered.

Cathy helped Dave with his business, but also worked at Michigan Maple Block in Petoskey. In her "spare" time, she canned vegetables from their garden, and cheered her kids in every activity in which they participated.

By the summer of 1994, however, Cathy began to show symptoms of slowing down. She became tired too easily and was feeling pressure in her chest, making it difficult to breathe at times. She had seen numerous doctors, none of whom seemed to know what was wrong.

Finally, one suggested they perform a hysterectomy to see if that would relieve the problem. Surgery was scheduled for October 1994.

That was the turning point that would bring Dave, Cathy and me together. We would recognize in each other very different personalities, but the same God at work in each. We would laugh and cry together as we learned to recognize God's hand in all events, even the ones that we might have scripted differently.

Most of all, we would come to know what it meant to be "faithful enough" that God could use each one of us in ministry and service.

Chapter

Even though I walk through the darkest valley,
I fear no evil; for you are with me. . .
—Psalm 23:4

The day before Cathy's surgery, a number of family members offered to sit with Dave while he waited at Northern Michigan Hospital. Being "tough Dave," the one who was always in control, Dave turned down every offer.

"Tough Dave" didn't count on finding someone tougher than him: eighty-one-year-old Harold Koteskey.

Dave had just settled into the hospital waiting room with one of their year-old magazines when Harold and his wife, Ruth, came through the door. "You mentioned last night that Cathy was having her surgery," Harold said, enveloping Dave's hand in his own. "I told Ruth when I got home, and we agreed we would come and wait with you today."

A retired minister, Harold had sold Dave his property under a land contract when the Cadarettes first arrived in Horton Bay. Once a month, Dave had gone to the Koteskeys' home to drop off a check, and usually stayed awhile to chat with the couple. Even after the land contract was paid off, Dave enjoyed stopping by the couple's home to visit.

As time passed in the waiting room, Dave appreciated the Koteskeys' presence, but hoped they wouldn't notice he was checking his watch every five minutes. Dave had been told Cathy's surgery would be finished by 11:00. The hour came—and went.

Dave continued to drink coffee and chat with the Koteskeys. By noon, most of the waiting room had cleared except for the trio and the volunteer wearing the pink jacket at the desk. Dave began to feel his stomach turn—not so much from hunger, but from that deep-down sense that something was very wrong.

At 1:00 P.M., the volunteer finally called Dave's name, and he hurried into the consulting room—the room from which so many before him emerged with relief and joy on their faces. Dave didn't expect good news. However, he wasn't prepared for what the doctors did tell him: Cathy's abdomen was filled with tumors.

"Mesothelioma. Incurable. Six months at the most."

Other words were said that day, but these were the ones Dave remembered. It was the words he numbly repeated to the Koteskeys as he returned to the waiting room.

To Harold and Ruth, it was as if one of their own children was struck by cancer. "We'll be praying for you," said Ruth, smothering Dave's much larger frame in one of her hugs.

Dave left the hospital and went home, but returned when he knew Cathy had awakened. Lying in the hospital bed, Cathy listened as the doctors repeated their prognosis.

"How could this be?" she asked, stunned. "How could this be happening to us?"

How indeed, Dave thought. How could he have only six more months with this woman he literally had loved at first sight? Dave had gone to a friend's party with a date, but as soon as he looked across the room, his eyes locked with Cathy's. He immediately knew this fifteen-year-old would one day be his wife. He took his date home, and returned to get to know this blond girl.

How could Cathy only have six more months with her husband of just twenty years? When they first talked about marriage, her mother objected that they were too young and immature. As if to prove her mother's point, Cathy and Dave devised a way to get married—they got Cathy pregnant. Her mother then consented, and seventeen-year-old Cathy became a wife and mother.

How could Dave and Cathy have only six more months as parents of their three children? Cathy had made their birthdays special and their holidays happy—all of their time together revolved around Cathy's love. How could they break the news to Amy, Brent and David?

"Don't tell the kids anything," Cathy told Dave as he prepared to go home. "I don't want us to tell them until we can do so together."

The next time Dave walked into the room, however, Cathy was crying. "I can't face the kids and tell them," she said. "Could you tell them alone?"

"I'll go home and tell the boys," Dave said.

After he left the hospital, however, Dave realized he couldn't find the words either. Instead of going inside, Dave headed into the woods behind their home—where he broke down in sobs.

"I'll do whatever you want, Lord," he called aloud to God. "I'll go to church; I'll read the Bible. Just give me the strength. Please help me."

Dave continued to weep as he tried to decide what God wanted of him. He didn't know much about church, but he thought of Ed and Ruth Chamberlain, members of Horton Bay United Methodist Church. About the same time Dave had reshingled the church, Dave had worked on the Chamberlains' home.

Dave remembered how, when he had been working at the Chamberlains, they often invited him to join them for lunch. A good Bohemian cook, Ruth wouldn't take no for an answer, even if Dave had tried to say it. Their meal around the kitchen table always began with the three joining hands and Ed saying grace.

Dave didn't know much about God, but as he knelt in the woods, he believed the Chamberlains might have some answers. He returned to his car, and headed to their home.

Ed and Ruth were surprised to see Dave, but immediately welcomed him into their two-story farmhouse. As Dave took a seat at the kitchen table where he had shared their meals, he could barely meet their eyes as he shared the news from the doctors.

Ed and Ruth listened with shock. Although they hadn't had many social encounters with Dave and Cathy, they had a real affection for them and their family.

The Chamberlains responded by telling Dave about Jesus. Ed, the son of a pastor, and Ruth had been brought up in church, and believed strongly in the love demonstrated by Jesus giving his life for all people.

The Chamberlains reminded Dave of all the people Jesus had healed in his lifetime, and how they believed healing—physical, spiritual and emotional—still came through God as revealed in Jesus.

"Would you pray with us?" Ed asked Dave, and then—as before—the Chamberlains and Dave joined hands around the kitchen table. Instead of offering a blessing over food, however, Ed prayed for blessings on Dave, Cathy and their family.

After he left their home, Dave was going to head home. Instead, he decided to visit the Koteskeys again. Maybe the Chamberlains didn't have all the answers; after all, they hadn't said anything about joining a church. Dave turned into the Koteskeys' driveway, wanting to make sure he wasn't missing anything.

So the next door to be opened to Dave was by Harold Koteskey. Dave again made himself at home in their kitchen, climbing onto one of the black barstools. No longer was he trying to be "tough Dave." Now, he allowed them to see him for what he truly was in that moment: an utterly broken man.

"Dave, do you know we love you and Jesus loves you?" Ruth asked him. "God wants to help you and Cathy through all of this."

The Koteskeys also offered to do one thing for Dave—like the Chamberlains, they pulled Dave into a circle with them, and they prayed with him.

As Harold prayed, Dave felt a new sense of peace—a sense that the burden he was carrying was now on the much-broader and stronger shoulders of God. Just as Koteskeys had insisted on coming to the wait with Dave at the hospital, Dave recognized that God was not letting him go this journey of faith alone.

As Dave prepared to leave, Ruth asked, "Do you have a Bible?" Dave confessed that they didn't have one in the house. They had sent their one copy with Amy when she went to college in Grand Rapids.

Digging out an extra copy of the *Everyday Bible*, Ruth gave it to Dave. "Take it home and start reading it," she said. "Now don't try to read it like a regular book. Try reading the book of John tonight."

Dave stifled a grin. He'd read maybe two books in his life, so reading it like a "regular book" meant little to him. However, he promised to read John that night and, with final hugs, went back out the door.

Chapter 3

Are any among you sick? They should call for the elders of the church and have them pray over them, anointing them with oil in the name of the Lord.
—James 5:14

Midway up the Koteskey driveway, I decided this was not one of my brighter ideas.

I was among a handful of people invited to Harold and Ruth's home that Sunday afternoon. Despite the calendar declaring it to be late November, the sun shining warmly through the parsonage windows convinced me it was still early autumn. As the Koteskeys lived directly behind my parsonage, my idea was to get some exercise by walking the half-mile driveway to their home.

Indeed, the sun was shining, but as I trudged along, I soon found a November wind was blowing. I pulled my head down into my coat, put my hands in my pockets for added warmth, and continued on my way until I heard gravel crunching behind me.

As I moved to the side of the driveway, Ed and Ruth Chamberlain's Subaru pulled alongside me. Ruth rolled down the passenger window. "Would you like to ride up to the house?" she asked.

"No, thanks," I said, not wanting them to think their pastor was a complete idiot. "I could stand the exercise."

With a wave, she and Ed drove on up the hill. I walked a few more feet, regretting that I'd declined the lift. By now, I was only halfway up the drive, and the trees to the left were no longer offering any protection from the wind.

Soon, I heard another vehicle behind me. Coming alongside me this time was Jan Leist, one of Cathy's best friends and my mail carrier. "Aren't you cold?" she asked, leaning over to speak to me through the window. "Jump in and I'll give you a ride the rest of the way."

Unfortunately, even a rookie pastor knows you *never* say no to one person's offer and then yes to an identical offer, unless you really want to offend someone. Therefore, I said again—with more shivers and less enthusiasm—"No, thanks. I could stand the exercise."

By the time I arrived, with my bright red nose and cheeks, at the Koteskeys, I'd made my best decision of the day: I would accept an offer of a ride home!

I soon thawed out, comforted as much by the furnace as I was by Harold and Ruth's hospitality. I found Dave and Cathy and their sons, Brent and David, had already arrived and taken seats on the Koteskeys' low overstuffed chairs.

Since Dave's visit with the Koteskeys after Cathy's surgery, he indeed had read the book of John as Ruth suggested. However, he'd continued reading more of the Bible. He and Cathy also had begun to attend worship services at Horton Bay along with their sons.

Still, I was grateful that Harold had offered this time together in which we would anoint Cathy. I hadn't had much interaction with the Koteskeys. Although the Horton Bay church was literally in their front yard, Harold and Ruth made the forty-five-minute drive each Sunday to the Ellsworth Wesleyan Church.

I did know that Harold, like most pastors, had a lead foot when it came to driving. Whether he was behind the wheel of his car, tractor, golf cart or dune buggy, Harold was always driving fast when he came motoring out the driveway alongside my kitchen windows.

At the same time, Harold was one of the slowest talkers I'd ever met. His measured pace would never fit into the sound bites of today's society. However, I noticed few people interrupted Harold or tried to finish his sentences. I think most people were like me; far from feeling impatient, I found reassurance and comfort in Harold's speech.

Harold had taken the initiative to ask Cathy whether she wished to be anointed with oil before her chemotherapy began.

Harold explained to Cathy that the book of James encourages those who are ill to gather with some church elders and be anointed with oil.

At seminary, our professors talked about offering anointing to those in need. I remember our seminary president telling us in one of our first sessions that Jesus called us to preach, teach and heal. If we didn't offer healing, he said, then we were hurting others.

However, the idea of anointing Cathy overwhelmed me. As I looked at her face, so full of expectation, I didn't want to inspire false hopes. Although I didn't know much about Harold, I felt that day his connection with the family would bring hope to them all.

After a few minutes of small talk, Harold brought us to the matter at hand. He brought out a small vial of olive oil and invited Cathy to kneel in the middle of the living room floor. Dave, Brent and David circled immediately around Cathy, and the rest of us fell behind them, reaching forward that we might touch Cathy's shoulders and head.

Cathy bowed her head as Harold reached out his aged fingers. Without any sign of trembling, he anointed Cathy's forehead. He too placed his hand on her head as he prayed for health and healing.

Maybe it was that measured voice, but Dave can remember to this day part of Harold's prayer on that November day: "Almighty God, we thank you for Cathy, and we pray for her healing. If it is your will, may you heal her completely of her cancer. And if it is not your will to provide physical healing, may she have three or four good years of life left to her."

What I remember of that day was Cathy's face as Harold's prayer ended. As we said our "amens," Cathy lifted up her head. I couldn't believe the sight—her face was filled with light and peace. I could tell at that moment, the burden of worry had been lifted from her shoulders—not from a false hope, but in faith and assurance.

No matter what happened after we left that warm house, Cathy realized God would be with her in sickness and in health. Cathy was filled with the spirit of hope which comes from the presence of God, and God alone.

Chapter

And remember, I am with you always,
to the end of the age.
—Matthew 28:20

On February 5, 1995, four Cadarettes stood before the altar rail at Horton Bay United Methodist Church. I baptized Brent and David Jr., and then Dave and Cathy responded with words to reaffirm the baptism vows made for them as children.

Dipping my hand again into the water basin and, pushing aside a strand of Cathy's wig, I made the sign of the cross on her forehead—just as Harold months before had anointed the same way in oil. "Remember your baptism, and be thankful," I said, as a droplet of water flowed down Cathy's forehead to mingle with her tears.

The feeling I have is so wonderful and great, Cathy wrote that day in her journal. *It was a very emotional experience for us. I was so very proud of my boys—all three of them.*

By this time, Cathy had received half of her chemo treatments. Doctors had encouraged her to keep a journal to record her emotions and her experiences, and to keep her spirit up.

Cathy had lost her honey-blond hair, and usually came to church wearing one of two wigs. The hair loss didn't seem to faze Cathy except that the wigs tended to make her scalp itch. When visiting Cathy in the comfort of her home, a guest would more often find her head topped with a colorful scarf than with one of the wigs.

On the other hand, another side effect really bothered her: the nausea. "I hate being sick," Cathy confessed before the treatments began. "I really don't want to be sick to my stomach."

But when Cathy received her first treatment, she became extremely ill. A couple of times, she returned to the hospital because she became dehydrated from vomiting.

With her second chemo treatment in December, Cathy received medications to help with the nausea. Unfortunately, Cathy never responded to prescriptions in the same way as most people. Whereas the directions for even common aspirin would prescribe two for a normal adult, Cathy found even half of one tablet was enough; any more would be an overdose for her system.

Dave would later tell the church, "Cathy's treatments were bad. Sometimes she did not know who she was or where she was. One day, I came to the room and found she had urinated on herself."

Despite the physical discomfort, one thing the chemo treatments couldn't touch was Cathy's sense of humor. "I concentrate on where the chemo is going, and visualize little Pac-mans eating all the cancer up," she would tell us at church prayer meetings.

With the hardship of the chemo, however, came the blessing of a new, stronger relationship with Dave. From the moment Dave had received the doctor's news about Cathy's condition, he became a new husband: one who suddenly realized what it was to serve.

"I learned how good a feeling it was to serve another," he told me. "I never helped with the dishes, the housework—I never had done any of that with Cathy until now. And now we can't do it together, because she is too sick. I wish I could have spent our other twenty years like we have the past one."

In learning to serve Cathy as she had served him, Dave realized how God serves us, and would have us serve one another. In service, Dave learned the true meaning of love—the love God has for us. That new love shined through him to Cathy as they endured six chemo treatments together.

At least a couple of times when I went to the hospital to check on Cathy, I walked into her room to find Cathy and Dave snuggled together in the tiny hospital bed. I'd turn quietly and tiptoe out of the room, hoping not to disturb them.

Dave couldn't always stay overnight. Realizing how much Cathy hated his absences, Dave bought a small pink teddy bear with "CATHY—I love you" printed on the front. He tucked the bear inside his shirt and kept it there the entire day. That night, as he kissed Cathy good-bye, he pulled the bear from under his shirt. Cathy hugged the bear all night, smelling Dave's scent even in his absence.

Cathy and Dave realized they were learning to communicate in way they never had dreamed possible. They began praying together aloud each night. Through Dave's prayers, Cathy realized Dave worried about a lot more than she had ever dreamed. In turn, she encouraged Dave to read her journal.

Dave went one step further—after reading Cathy's journal entry for the day, he wrote his own thoughts to his wife:

I know I haven't talked much about your cancer, Dave wrote. *But as I have been going through these times of troubles, I had been thinking that if I talk about or even consider the worse, that it may show doubt in my faith in God, and He may not answer my prayers and heal you, and let me live a long life with you.*

But as I walk and learn about my feelings and God's and follow his lead, I know now that whether or not He heals you that we'll always be together. I will always have your love and you will always have mine. If you die or if I die in five years or fifty, I truly believe we'll always be together and will always be.

As May 1995 approached, the chemo treatments couldn't weaken Cathy's proud smile as she watched Amy cross the graduation platform at Aquinas College in Grand Rapids. Weeks later, the same proud smile lit up the gymnasium at Boyne City High School as Brent received his own diploma. The day after Brent's reception, Cathy had her final chemo treatment.

One month later, Cathy and Dave sat across from their doctor, ready to hear his report. They braced themselves for the news they expected, the news so many other patients had heard: that the chemo was ineffective and the cancer was continuing to grow. Instead, the doctor delivered unbelievable news.

The CAT scan showed nothing, Cathy wrote in her journal that night. *Even the spot on my lungs is down. Dr. D said they stopped the cancer from growing. He doesn't know if it will grow again. We only have to wait and see. He was pleased, and so was Dave and I!! God has truly heard our prayers!*

Life seems so more meaningful now!! It is a pleasure to get up in the morning and go to work!! I am not stopping praying for me not to get this back, though. I don't ever want to go through that again—but if I have to, I will.

Chapter

I am about to do a new thing.
—Isaiah 43:19

Those entering Horton Bay church one fall evening were startled as Jim Ledahl greeted them, resplendent in full black cape. "Good evening," he intoned in a deep bass voice, which is to say his normal voice. "Kindly step into the *dead* center of the room."

OK, not the usual greeting for those being welcomed to Horton Bay church. However, this was not a usual Sunday service. Black and orange crepe paper decorated the room, and Macintosh apples bobbed in the large metal wash pan. On this October night in 1995, Horton Bay prepared to host its first fall festival.

I grinned as the children arrived in homemade costumes. Although adults were "allowed" to wear costumes, most of us opted for casual clothes for the evening.

Therefore, I was a little disconcerted to notice a strange woman coming through the front door, looking as if she were arriving for Sunday morning services. She wore a bright purple and blue dress, full makeup and high heels.

What made the sight more surprising was the sight behind her: a scruffy-looking man. True, he had on a black suit, tie and hat, but the day's growth of beard made him look more like an Emmett Kelly-hobo than a gentleman dressed for church.

As they came near me, I struggled to recall their names. I couldn't believe any strangers would choose Halloween as their introduction to the church. And something was vaguely familiar about that woman as she sashayed into Fellowship Hall with a big grin on her face.

Then I realized: that was no woman grinning at me. That "woman" was Dave Cadarette, and the scruffy-looking man was Cathy.

"You were so convincing as a woman," we told Dave. "How could you walk in those high heels?"

"I've watched more than a few women from the rear!" Dave admitted.

Almost a year had passed since Dave and Cathy had first walked through the doors of our church. Their arrival had offered Horton Bay a chance to test its definition of itself as a "friendly, family church."

That was the definition church officers gave when I had first arrived at Horton Bay—a definition that made me nervous. "Friendly, family church" often translates as a small congregation friendly to everyone within its walls, but suspicious of newcomers. In fact, many members of a "friendly, family church" will take time Sunday mornings to greet all the other members, but not offer even a handshake or smile to a newcomer.

I well remembered Dave and Cathy's first Sunday at church. They couldn't have chosen a worse day for their introduction to our services. Instead of the usual morning worship, we conducted our annual church conference, a time to review our work in 1994 and to approve the officers and budget for the coming year. In other words, boring.

When the Cadarettes introduced themselves to me that morning, I almost blanched. I figured anyone seeking a church home that Sunday would be looking in another church the following week.

But the Cadarettes had returned the following Sunday, and almost every Sunday since. During the prayer concerns, they shared the news of Cathy's cancer with the congregation, and asked that people begin praying for them. Ed and Ruth Chamberlain made a point of introducing them to as many people as they could, and soon all of the members knew the Cadarette family members by name.

Between the time of those first Sundays and the "cross-dress-ing" incident at the Fall Festival, Horton Bay had begun to redefine "friendly, family church." To members, friendly came to mean reaching out to more than those they knew—it meant extending a greeting to anyone who had a need, be it spiritual, physical or emotional.

And family no longer meant ties to relatives alone. Family meant anyone, period.

As Cathy underwent chemo, members supplied full meals to the family so Cathy wouldn't worry about cooking meals. Many Sundays, the Cadarettes would fill an entire table in Fellowship Hall with empty, clean casserole dishes needing to be returned to church members.

Dave and Cathy also began attending Bible study on Sunday and Wednesday evenings at Horton Bay. Many long-time attendees would nod their heads approvingly as Ed Chamberlain or other Sunday school teachers would use words like "justification," "sanctification" and "eschatology" without definition, because they knew what the words meant—or maybe they had just heard preachers use them so often, they knew they were important words.

Not any more. Anyone trying to use good-sounding theological terms would be interrupted. "What does that mean?" Cathy would ask. And sometimes after getting a definition, she'd turn to me and insist, "But what does it *mean*?"

Not only did she demand definitions, Cathy and Dave would ask why people acted in a manner they defined as Christian. For example, many of our "old school" members had a very strict interpretation of Sabbath rest. On Sundays, they not only wouldn't patronize restaurants; they would go home to precooked meals so no work was done to prepare a Sunday dinner.

The Cadarettes would question this kind of conduct, not as a challenge, but rather so they could understand how church members defined "Christian." In return, those being questioned took the opportunity to reexamine their own ways and beliefs, instead of just answering, "Because that's how my dad/grandfather did it."

For Cathy, the most asked question was, "But what has all of this to do with the way I live my life?" Never mind that I had just delivered a sermon or Bible study that would make theologians take notes. I knew if the message had no practical application in her life,

Cathy would hold up the entire greeting line until she was satisfied with a practical explanation of what I'd just said.

And around Cathy, I didn't feel like being a serious-sounding theologian. When I'd first arrived at Horton Bay, the elders asked what I'd like to be called. They insisted I should have a formal title, so that the children would view me with respect.

From day one, I was called Pastor Kathy—until Cathy came along. She began calling me "P.K." for short, and the nickname began to catch on with other people.

One other change in the congregation became noticeable. When I had arrived at Horton Bay, I found that the congregation enjoyed giving verbal prayer concerns and praises. However, almost every Sunday, the same people would speak, and they almost always had something to say about problems in their lives.

After Cathy and Dave became members, however, I found each Sunday morning I'd be looking in their direction, knowing one or the other—or both—would speak during prayer time. Instead of sitting and directing their words to me, they would stand in their pew and face the congregation. They were as apt to share praises for a good garden as they were to talk of a struggles in their faith that week.

"Do you think we say too much in church?" Cathy asked me on more than one occasion.

"That depends," I said. "Are you standing up and speaking because you think the people want you to?"

"No," she said. "Dave and I *hate* public speaking. But it seems like every Sunday, the Spirit moves us to share something with the congregation."

"Then as long as what you say is from the heart," I responded, "you are saying what needs to be heard."

Our prayer time slowly grew from a few words to up to twenty minutes in which people shared. Those who had never offered a word during worship would unabashedly tell of the things God was doing in their lives. Their praises came as frequently as the concerns, and the depth of those concerns began to spread beyond our four walls, encompassing persons around the world.

Many of the prayer concerns and praises shared by others brought tears to Cathy's eyes. Like me, she could cry at a sentimental

Hallmark commercial. Unlike me, she had no inhibition about hiding those tears during services.

I was straightening hymns in the pews one day when I noticed a strange box on the end of the row where Cathy regularly sat. The brown and white checkerboard box was two inches wide and a foot long. I opened it up to find it full of neatly folded Kleenex.

"What is this?" I asked Cathy the next time I saw her.

"Oh, that's from Vera Hallman," she said, naming a neighbor and a friend who usually sat in the pew with Cathy's family. "She brought that so I would have Kleenex whenever I cry."

From then on, the narrow box became a permanent fixture in their pew, with Vera refilling it as needed. As for the Cadarettes, they seemed to fill and refill the entire church congregation with a new sense of mission, hope and purpose. God was indeed creating a "new thing" at Horton Bay United Methodist Church: a thing of beauty and joy.

Chapter

We speak of these things in words not taught by human wisdom, but taught by the Spirit.
—I Corinthians 2:13

One of Cathy's frequent praises at Horton Bay United Methodist Church was for Dave's "direct line to God." From those first moments Dave knelt alone in the woods, Dave felt the Holy Spirit give him messages he knew could only come from God.

Sometimes that close connection evoked envy in Cathy. On at least one occasion, however, the connection was something both Cathy and Dave would offer in praise of God.

It happened one summer day when Dave accompanied Cathy to a doctor's appointment in Petoskey. There, they bumped into the mother-in-law of their friend, Bill.

Bill, an alcoholic, had been struggling with his addiction without success. Through the past months, Dave shared what had been happening in his life and in Cathy's. He gave Bill some books and spoke to Bill's wife, but nothing seemed to ease Bill's pain.

Now, his mother-in-law told them Bill had left a suicide note. His family believed he was in Boyne Falls, but did not know his location.

Boyne Falls is bigger than Horton Bay, but not by much. Located on the foot of Boyne Mountain, a major ski resort, Boyne Falls is one of those towns most people go through to get elsewhere—unless they're going to the annual Boyne Falls Polish Festival. Because of its proximity to the Mountain, however, there were a number of motels and inns where Bill could have chosen to stay.

After Dave and Cathy parted outside the hospital, Dave realized God was using His "direct line" to tell Dave to go to Boyne Falls. The Holy Spirit was telling Dave that God needed him to intervene with Bill, and tell him of God's love.

But Dave had a few things to tell God: "No, I can't go," he said aloud in his truck. "I've got two or three guys working in Harbor Springs waiting for materials, and two in Boyne City waiting for materials. I'm spending over $100 an hour in wages, and I can't afford to take time off now."

Dave left the hospital and drove just a few blocks south to Preston Feather Building Center. He loaded shingles and lumber onto the truck, and then pulled to the end of the driveway—and couldn't get out.

Traffic snarls in Petoskey are commonplace in the summer months. However, for five minutes, Dave sat waiting for traffic to clear. He wanted to pull onto U.S. 131 and head north—the exact opposite direction from Boyne Falls. As he waited, he continued to argue with God. Each time God told him, "Go to Boyne Falls," Dave kept saying, "I can't. I can't. I've got too much to do."

For another five minutes, Dave waited without any break in the traffic. Finally, he said, "All right! I'll go."

The second he said, "All right," three things happened. Dave felt as if he had been dipped in formaldehyde—he was chilled to the bone. Second, God told Dave which motel Bill was in—and that he was in Room 6. And third, the traffic cleared. Dave headed south to Boyne Falls.

As he pulled into Boyne Falls, Dave decided to drive past the motel he believed Bill to be in, just to see if Bill's vehicle was in sight. Sure enough, as Dave passed the motel, he saw Bill's truck parked outside Room 6. Now positive that God—and God alone—could have given him this wisdom, Dave returned to the motel, pulled along Bill's truck, and went to knock on the door at Room 6.

Dave didn't have a clue what to say to his friend, but he figured if God could bring him all the way down from Petoskey, God could give him the right words to say.

When Bill answered the door, Dave started with, "How are things going?"

"How does it look like they're going?" Bill asked.

"Not very well," Dave replied, as Bill let him into the motel room.

As he sat down, Dave knew what to say. "Bill, I can't help you, but I brought somebody who can," he said. "I brought God with me."

Dave then explained how God had let Dave know exactly where Bill was, and then blocked Dave's "exit route" until Dave was willing to go to Boyne Falls.

Surely a God who wouldn't take Dave's "no" for an answer was a God who loved Bill as much as any of His children. God didn't share wisdom with Dave for the sake of Dave looking good; God shared His wisdom that Bill might know God loved him, too.

To this, Bill responded. He prayed with Dave, accepting Jesus as his Savior. He admitted to Dave he'd planned to kill himself the night before in that motel room, but God stopped him. And with Dave's help, Bill recognized God as being "a very present help," there to give Bill strength to recover, and strength for new life.

Dave shared this story with us at the next Wednesday evening service. "I'm beginning to learn," Dave admitted, with a wry sense of humor and wonder at the same time, "that sometimes God needs to use a two-by-four to get my attention. But when He does, boy, does He have all the answers I need."

7

Chapter

The apostles said to the Lord, "Increase our faith!"
The Lord replied, "If you had faith the size of a
mustard seed, you could say to this mulberry tree, 'Be
uprooted and planted in the sea,' and it would obey you."
—Luke 17:5-7

Good pastors learn to look for the bad on Sunday mornings. The good is easy to find. As pastors greet parishioners after the service, they become accustomed to hearing "good sermon," "I'm doing good," etc., all in a good tone of voice.

What I learned was more important was to be aware of the bad: the bad tone of voice, the person who avoids eye contact, the person who responds to "how are you" with a slow "okay," or even a "not so good." The challenge was there every Sunday to recognize the person who needed to talk, but wasn't willing to directly tell me.

On Palm Sunday 1996, Cathy was that person. What she said to me after morning worship was, "We need to talk some day." She didn't give any clue as to what she wanted to discuss, but I could tell from her tone of voice that "someday" needed to be soon. I called her that afternoon and arranged to meet Tuesday for lunch at Wendy's in Petoskey.

Unbeknownst to me that day, Cathy wrote in her journal, *I should be the happiest person in the world right now, but I'm not. I am very depressed. And I really don't know why. I have a lot of bad thoughts these days. About dying, cancer, bad memories. I try so hard to push them out of my mind. I've asked God to lift me up and drive the bad thoughts out of my mind.*

I know I have to put more faith in God, but I'm not really sure how to do that. I think I am at times, and other times I'm just not sure. I don't like feeling the doubt. I wish I could be sure of myself as Dave is of himself.

On Tuesday, I arrived at Wendy's first, and settled down at a table a little removed from where most people were eating. I don't usually choose such open places for counseling, but the restaurant was close to Cathy's work. Her employer, Michigan Maple Block, had been more than generous in paying Cathy even when she had been too sick to work, and she tried to repay her employer by being as conscientious as possible about her hours while she was healthy.

Cathy soon arrived, got her own meal and joined me. After munching on a few fries and dispensing with the usual chitchat, Cathy looked directly at me as her eyes filled with tears.

"P.K., I don't want to die," she said. She quickly added, "I'm not afraid to die because I know I will be with the Lord. That's not it. I'm afraid of leaving my family alone—of not being able to watch the kids grow up and marry or whatever. I want to grow old with Dave together."

"Cathy, you've learned so much in the past two years," I said. "One of those things is how precious this life is. You've said many times you don't ever want to take one moment for granted again. Now that you've faced death, you've had time to realize what your family and your life mean to you. There's nothing wrong with admitting how much you would miss them."

After a pause, she added, "I just need more faith. How do I get more faith?"

After a pause myself, I asked, "Just how much faith do you need?"

I love answering questions with a question. Facing my question usually makes parishioners realize pastors don't have all the answers. I think it also encourages them to draw from their own reason and abilities to come to the answers.

I saw it happen in Cathy's face that day: the dawning light on her face as she sat up a little straighter. "I guess I don't need more faith,"

Cathy said. "You either have faith or you don't, and I know that I do." I could tell from her face she was digesting this more fully, and kept quiet as I watched her.

I also marveled at her sense that her faith was small. How could she possibly not know how her journey of faith was inspiring so many others at Horton Bay? So often, she confessed she wished she could pray like Ed Chamberlain. Surely she knew that Ed wished he could pray in her simple, honest style!

"It's just," Cathy began anew, "Dave seems to be able to hear God speak directly to him. Dave tells me all the time that God tells him I will be all right. But I don't hear God giving me that message. I just wish God would let me know that He hears me."

"Well, we all have our way of talking with God and hearing God's answers," I said. "Dave's way doesn't have to be your way, nor does it have to be mine. God chose to respond to people in the Bible in a variety of ways. I presume He still does so."

"Is it OK to ask God for a sign?" Cathy asked.

"It depends," I said. "The Bible says we're not supposed to test God, and in a few places, Jesus refused to do any signs for the people. Most of the time, it was because God knew people would remember the sign, but forget the one who gave it.

"On the other hand, God has allowed people to ask for signs. Do you remember Gideon? He asked God for a very specific sign to verify what God was asking of him. God gave the sign—which prompted Gideon to ask for another sign. And God answered that one, too, without chastising Gideon for being weak."

I looked across at Cathy. Her hair had returned to its usual thickness and length, but was now more brunette than blond. This person had become such a good friend, and I felt so inadequate answering her questions. I may have been to seminary, but I had spent only one night in a hospital, and that was for tonsils when I was five years old. My answers might have satisfied a religion scholar, but I felt I wasn't quite reaching Cathy.

Our lunch hour was up, and Cathy and I began placing trash on our trays and digging in our purses for our car keys. A smiling hostess came to our table and politely asked if she could take our trays.

Then the hostess caught sight of Cathy's bracelet, a piece of cloth with white letters WWJD—What Would Jesus Do? "I really like those," she said. "It makes me pause to think about what I should do myself, although I sometimes wonder what Jesus *would* do."

"You should have joined us," Cathy said, as she and I stood up and prepared to leave. "This is my pastor, and we've been having a conversation on faith."

"I just recently became a born again Christian," the woman said. "I really started going back to church after I got cancer."

I glanced at Cathy. She had stopped gathering her coat, and was giving her full attention to the woman. "I also have cancer," Cathy said. "I'm in remission right now, but I have so many questions about God and whether I'm going to be OK."

"I was told I had only a few months when I was first diagnosed, and that was a couple of years ago," the woman said. "I wouldn't ever want to go through the chemo again, but only by becoming ill did I turn to God and become saved. I wouldn't trade that for anything."

"How do you know that you won't get sick again?" Cathy asked.

"I don't," the woman replied. "I just know God will be as faithful with me in the future as He has in the past, and for now, that's enough to answer all my questions."

Suddenly, Cathy and I knew—God was providing her sign. Of all the people we could have met in this place at this time, God provided an angel—a messenger—who had been through Cathy's circumstances and could answer her questions much better than I. It was a sign that God did hear Cathy, and did respond.

The next time I saw Cathy, she told me she went back to Wendy's the next day to thank the hostess for her words. "Actually, I was a little nervous," she said. "I thought it might be like on *Touched by an Angel,* and maybe she never really worked there, but was just put there by God for us to see."

However, Cathy found indeed it was a very real human at work. Cathy expressed her thanks to the woman, and shared how her words had helped Cathy in her struggle. "She told me she's seeking a new job as a hostess in a local homeless shelter," Cathy told me.

What Cathy wrote in her journal that night was, *I truly believe she was an angel answering some of my questions. I prayed for her to get the job she was longing for. I pray for a lot of things—I hope not too much. I know God listens to me!!*

Chapter 8

And now faith, hope, and love abide, these three;
and the greatest of these is love.

—I Corinthians 13:13

As people settled in their pews for the first midweek service of 1996, Cathy piped up: "I'm going to be a mother-in-law!"

On New Year's Eve, Eric Smith had proposed to Amy. Cathy immediately began telling friends, family and fellow employees. "Some people thought I was telling them I was going to be a grandmother," Cathy said with glee. "They said they'd never heard anyone get so excited about being an in-law."

Even as we celebrated in that first evening, however, Cathy admitted to the Bible study group at Horton Bay that she was having some difficulty with the idea of "letting go" of her daughter. Never mind that Amy was twenty-two years old, living and working three hours away in Grand Rapids. She and her mother spoke almost daily on the phone and had a very close mother-daughter relationship.

"I don't like this phrase, 'Who gives this woman,'" Cathy told our group. Turning to me, she seriously said, "P.K., couldn't you ask, 'Who loans this woman,' or 'Who shares this woman?'"

Our group pointed out that the Bible says those whom God has joined together, let no one—not even a mother-in-law—separate. Cathy wasn't satisfied. Even the old saying "a daughter's a daughter all of her life" didn't appease Cathy's fear that she was losing a best friend.

Cathy also worried about the expenses she and Dave would have in the wedding. Dave, of course, kept telling her to have faith; yet she wrote in her journal many times about her concern about raising their share of the finances for the wedding and reception.

And, in the midst of their planning, Cathy's cancer returned. *I feel something in my right lung,* she wrote on June 18. *It hurts when I breathe real deep or I sneeze. I'm going in for another CAT scan on 7-9-96, then a week later I will see the doctor. I hope there is nothing there. If nothing shows up, I will ask the doc to do more tests. Something is not right.*

The CAT scan indeed revealed new growth in the tumors in Cathy's abdomen, plus something else: breast cancer. With the nearness of the wedding, Cathy was willing to have surgery to remove the spot in her breast. However, she decided to delay chemo and radiation for the mesothelioma until after Christmas.

Cathy's surgery took place without any problems. By Labor Day weekend, she still was fighting some fatigue from the anesthesia, but was all smiles at the rehearsal at Boyne City United Methodist Church. Dave and Cathy hated not having the wedding at Horton Bay, but the greater seating capacity of Boyne City was needed to accommodate the guests.

Gathering Eric and Amy in front of me, I invited everyone into a word of prayer as we recognized the holiness of the upcoming wedding. I prayed, "Lord, please bless this new family you are creating of Eric and Cathy…. Um, Amy…." Suddenly, the mother of the bride had company in her nervousness. I made a mental note to put some sticky notes with the right names in my *Book of Worship*.

As the rehearsal progressed, I also made a mental note to remind Dave before he walked Amy down the aisle, he really needed to spit out his chewing gum. I'd never noticed him chewing gum in other places, but at rehearsal, he was chewing gum as fast as his jaw could move—a sign that Cathy wasn't the only one feeling they were losing a daughter.

The next morning, I called the Cadarettes to see if anyone had last-minute questions. Cathy told me Amy had a peculiar dream the night before in which I was supposed to be getting ready for the wedding, but instead mowed the yard. Using one of those old-fashioned push mowers, I soon was showered with grass clippings that clung to my face like whiskers.

Before Amy arrived at the church, I took the outside rim of a paper plate, smeared it with glue, and put it down in the mowed grass of the churchyard. When Amy walked in the door, I turned around with my grass beard under my chin. "I just can't imagine why you were having bad dreams," I said, as she shook her head in disbelief.

I'd hoped in doing this, the tension every bride feels would be abated. Amy would calm down for a few minutes until another family member would come to check on her, and break into tears at the sight of her in her wedding dress—making Amy nervous all over again.

Cathy tried not to show her own nervousness, and instead talked about how uncomfortable she was in a dress. At Horton Bay, Cathy almost always wore slacks. This was one of the rare occasions I saw her not only in a beautiful mint-green dress, but also in makeup—which she'd borrowed from friends.

Finally, I sent Amy and Dave upstairs to prepare for their entrance. As they waited for Ruth Chamberlain to play *Here Comes the Bride,* Amy felt all of her tension melt away, and she was sure God's presence was filling her with peace.

Cathy's brown and white checkerboard box of Kleenex had been transferred to her front pew in the Boyne City church. She wondered how long she could hold off before reaching for her first tissue, but the rest of the wedding party knew. As Dave escorted Amy to the end of the aisle, they came alongside Cathy in the front pew. Amy pulled a small section from her wedding bouquet, leaned over and handed the nosegay to Cathy. Tears immediately began to flow.

As Amy came to stand in front of me, I announced, "Friends, we are gathered together in the sight of God to witness and bless the joining together of Eric and *Amy* in Christian marriage."

As I glanced up at the couple before me, I realized Eric was sweating. Not nervous beads of sweat. Eric looked as if he'd been playing full-press basketball for a solid hour. I glanced at the others at the altar rail to see whether the heat was getting to them. Everyone else looked fine.

Still, I didn't desire to have a six-foot-plus groom fainting before the entire congregation, so I shortened my sermon considerably. Encouraging Eric and Amy to face each other, I had them give their vows, and sent them back up the aisle as husband and wife.

She was the most beautiful bride in the world, Cathy wrote in her journal. *Brent and David were so handsome in their tuxes. And Dave was the perfect father of the bride. Everything went wonderful. We were able to pay for the wedding without going into debt.*

I thanked God and only God for that. Dave keeps telling me to have more faith. I think I do, but I still worry about things.

Chapter

Beloved, let us love one another, because love is from God; everyone who loves is born of God and knows God.
—I John 4:7

A few days before Cathy was to start her second round of chemo, she sat in the family room watching television. Dave had disappeared into the bathroom for a long time, but Cathy didn't think much of it.

Finally, Dave came around the corner and presented Cathy with a present: his gleaming, bald head. Dave knew Cathy would soon be losing her hair from the chemo. As a gesture of love and support, Dave had shaved his own head.

"I wanted to make you feel better, knowing you wouldn't be alone," he said, beaming from ear to ear—and also beaming overhead from ear to ear.

But the gift backfired. "You look awful!" Cathy cried. "If I'm going to look that ridiculous, I feel terrible!" Then grinning herself, she added, "It's a wonderful gesture, honey, but don't ever do that again."

For Cathy's second round of chemo, the doctors decided to try a new kind of treatment. Others with the tumors caused by mesothelioma had responded well.

Cathy's response was one of fatigue. *I seem to be very weak from this chemo,* she wrote. *Don't seem to be springing back as fast as I would like to.*

I will try to go to work tomorrow. They have been really good to me!! I'm just tired. I try to do things around the house so Dave doesn't have to. I feel so guilty with him doing everything. God has truly blessed him with patience. He's been a saint thru all this, as well as the boys and Amy. I had to remind myself that they are affected by this as much as I am.

As with the first round of chemo, Cathy was scheduled to undergo six treatments in approximately six months. About midway through, however, she noticed side effects more disturbing than hair loss.

For one thing, she began to have trouble hearing. After the treatments, Cathy regained some of her sense, but she had to strain to catch most high-pitched sounds—including my voice. I found I needed to lower the tenor of my voice when we talked, so she could pick up the words.

More permanent was nerve damage in Cathy's hands and feet. When she and Dave quizzed the doctors, they learned this was a common side effect. However, Cathy, Dave and their doctor felt it was too destructive to Cathy's body, and stopped treatments after four doses.

To their relief, tests showed the four doses had stopped the growth of the tumors in Cathy's abdomen. "I'm OK, I'm going to be OK," Cathy announced with joy on a Sunday morning, as many in the congregation applauded.

By March 1997, Cathy had recovered her strength enough to go on a trip to Florida with her friend, Jan Leist. It was the first real vacation Cathy had ever taken. Even as they boarded the plane, Cathy was coming up with reasons why she should stay home with family.

As soon as the plane door was locked however, Cathy turned to Jan. "Thank you for talking me into this," she said.

The two visited the Tampa Bay area of Florida, visiting Jan's family and doing the usual sightseeing. Despite all the seashell shops, Cathy was determined to find a sand dollar on the beach—and succeeded.

As soon as they got home, Cathy had all her film developed, and showed Dave pictures of her walking in the sand, sitting in the sunshine, and even posing at Busch Gardens with a bright red bird on top of her head. As Cathy showed the photos to Dave, he commented, "You're smiling in every single picture."

Cathy soon threw herself into duties as lay leader for Horton Bay church. When I had asked her to consider this job, her first question was, "What does the lay leader do?"

"Quite frankly, not much," I answered. "The church hasn't had anyone serve as lay leader for some years. You're supposed to encourage every member of the church to do ministry in some manner. Other than that, I really don't have a practical job description for you."

So Cathy and I made one up. First in her responsibilities was to find a liturgist for each Sunday service. I had warned Horton Bay when I arrived as pastor that I didn't believe the pastor should rule over the worship service. I began to choose a member of the congregation to help me each week with the service, including reading the morning's scripture lessons.

Unfortunately, most people I asked were quick to turn me down. "Oh, you read so well," they'd protest, cutting off my invitation. "I'm not half the professional that you are." As a result, I had only four people who regularly served as liturgist.

Once Cathy became lay leader, however, those protests met a brick wall. "Well, what the heck do you think I am?" Cathy would say. "I'm just like you, and I've made my mistakes. Remember the time I announced that although the New Revised Standard Bible was in the pews, I would be reading from a different 'transmission' instead of 'translation?'"

As soon as the two would stop laughing, Cathy would say, "So, I'll just put you down for this Sunday, OK?"

Cathy gave liturgists the scripture a few days in advance so they'd have plenty of time to practice. She had one very practical tip for Dave before a Christmas Eve service. "Mary was Joseph's espoused wife, not his exposed wife," she said, correcting his reading of Luke 2:5.

Also as lay leader, Cathy became responsible for attending to the spiritual nourishment of the congregation. To attend to her own development, Cathy signed up for the Fall 1997 Win-Some Women's Retreat at Boyne Mountain. Almost a thousand women from eighty communities came together each year for a weekend of inspirational speakers, prayer and spiritual nourishment. Ruth Koteskey served on the steering committee and, this year, I led the sunrise prayer time. Between Ruth and me, we persuaded Cathy to attend.

Many of the sessions were small-group format. However, our meals and keynote speakers brought all of the participants into the 950-capacity General Assembly Meeting Hall. The second day, I was seated with Cathy when the leader suggested we sing *Jesus Loves Me* to prepare for the afternoon. The familiar tune soon was lifted up in almost exclusively soprano and alto tones.

As we began the chorus of "Yes, Jesus loves me," however, one voice dropped out. Cathy stopped singing and stood up. By now, women were changing from unison to harmony, and the song reverberated throughout the room.

Cathy continued to stand, oblivious to others who glanced her way. Her eyes were closed, her face transfixed by the music. As the last notes died, she sat down again, but the smile wouldn't leave her face.

"I may have looked funny," she confessed the next morning in church, "but it was so beautiful, I couldn't sing—I just had to listen."

Dave too was attending to his spiritual development. He began attending the annual Promise Keepers' conventions in Detroit and, in the fall of 1997, flew to Washington D.C. for the national rally.

Individually and as a couple, Dave and Cathy continued to grow stronger each day. They would need to, for 1998 was on the horizon.

Chapter

My soul waits for the Lord more than those
who watch for the morning, more than those who
watch for the morning.
—Psalm 130:6

Usually, the firstborn son receives his father's name if the couple is going to have a "junior" in the family. Dave and Cathy were not a usual couple.

"Don't you realize how much trouble you'll have later if he has your name?" Cathy said when their first son was born. Dave agreed, and they named their first son Brent.

When their second son was born, however, Cathy relented. By the time David Jr. reached his senior year in high school, however, Cathy's prophecy was coming true.

"I can't call him Davey anymore," she said to me, "because that's too childish. I can't use Dave for both of them, because no one knows who I'm talking to. I used to use big Dave and little Dave, but now little Dave is bigger than big Dave! And old and young Dave just doesn't sound right."

So it was that Cathy came up with the solution most of us adopted in the fall of 1997: We referred to her husband as Dave, and her son as David.

David was the one who asked his mother in October what she wanted for her birthday. Cathy responded with the universal mother answer, "Nothing."

"No, come on," David insisted. "What would you like?"

"I'd like for my family to be together," Cathy replied wistfully. It seemed impossible with David in school, Brent involved in his activities, and Amy and Eric living in Grand Rapids.

As Cathy arrived home that Friday, the feelings were reinforced. With so many people in her family, only one vehicle was evident—Dave's. Although Cathy appreciated their relationship, she missed her kids. As she crossed the driveway, she was overwhelmed with "empty nest" syndrome.

As she entered the house, however, she was overwhelmed by something else: the smell of cabbage. "I love cabbage," she said Sunday as she told the church of her experience. "But I thought, what is Dave doing fixing cabbage for the two of us?

"I went around the corner—and there was my family. Everyone had come together for dinner."

It was good for the family to be together as Dave and Cathy were facing some tough times. Always an animal lover, Cathy had received a Pomeranian the previous Christmas. Suzie had been her inseparable companion. Frequently during the summer, I'd looked out the parsonage window in time to see Cathy zip by in her golf cart, Suzie happily in her lap.

Not that Suzie was exclusively Cathy's dog. On a trip to Grand Rapids, Dave and Cathy realized Suzie needed to go to the bathroom. Dave pulled the car over alongside U.S. 131 and stopped by some trees.

However, rain had soaked the ground adjacent to the roadway, and Suzie wanted nothing to do with stepping on the wet surface. As Cathy sat in the car and laughed, Dave carried Suzie back into the woods where he found a clear dry spot, and put the dog down to do her business.

One fall night, however, I answered a knock on the parsonage door to find Dave standing sober-faced before me. I braced for news about Cathy. Instead, Dave said, "Could you come out to the car and speak to Cathy? Some neighborhood dogs attacked and killed Suzie."

I came around the passenger side of the car to find Cathy crying uncontrollably. "How could this happen?" she asked. I realized I was adding in my own thoughts, "How could this happen to a family who's already gone through so much?"

Dave dug a grave behind the family's house. As he prepared to bury Suzie, he first lifted her up in his arms, giving her back to God. As he did so, an incredible sense of peace filled him.

As fall turned to winter, Dave and Cathy were considering an experimental treatment being tried on the East Coast for patients with mesothelioma. Talc, such as is found in talcum powder, is inserted into the abdomen, and causes the lungs to adhere directly to the chest cavity. This limits the area where tumors can develop and grow.

Dave and Cathy discussed whether she should undergo the procedure. To do so would mean flying to Boston and the cost, while not prohibitive, certainly was a consideration. After asking the church to pray for discernment, they opted not to go to Boston.

On Dec. 8, 1997, Cathy took time to write in her journal. Thirteen months had passed since her last entry, so she did some catching up. *It was a wonderful summer, beautiful weather and a good garden. Good thing Dave and God have a green thumb!*

David is a senior now. He broke his hand the first football game. Got infection & was in the hospital for 13 days!! Medication for almost 8 weeks. It's almost over now! He is planning to move to Ann Arbor to play hockey on an AA hockey team. I hope all goes well.

We have a new Pom: Hailey!! She's my baby girl puppy. She brings a lot of joy to us!!

Amy & Eric have a chocolate Lab named Cali. They figure if they can get thru the puppy stage that they can make it thru the baby stage?!?

Brent has had a tough year. I have been praying for him a lot. He works so hard that sometimes he doesn't use his head when he makes some decisions. But I think he's learning by his mistakes. I love him so!!

I have had an endoscopy done in my abdomen, and things did not look good: Dr. Wilcox said that everything was covered with tumors. I got very depressed.

My true feelings—I gave up after he told me. I actually gave up. I talked to Ruth K. and she assures me that it is very human of me to have these feelings. I am very embarrassed to say how I feel. But I talked to Dr. D on Tuesday and we are going to start some chemo on Jan. 6. It has showed good results on shrinking my kind of cancer.

So God pulled me out of my hole!! Thanks to him. I have hope again.—will write soon.

It was the last entry she ever made.

Chapter 11

When you pass through the waters, I will be with you;
and through the rivers, they shall not overwhelm you;
when you walk through the fire you shall not be burned,
and the flame shall not consume you.

—Isaiah 42:2

D ave began to dread the question from Cathy.

Since she had first been diagnosed with cancer, Cathy asked on a regular basis: "Dave, am I going to be all right? What does God tell you?" For three years, Dave had the same answer for Cathy: Whenever Dave prayed, he felt God would tell him Cathy was going to be all right.

By February 1998, however, when Dave asked God how Cathy was going to be, the reply was silence. God didn't say Cathy was going to die, but neither did God assure Dave that Cathy was going to be all right.

Maybe God didn't want Dave to misinterpret what "all right" would mean. Maybe God was telling Dave the answer and Dave chose not to hear; maybe God was silent because God knew Dave wasn't ready for the answer.

But as soon as God's silence began, Dave began his own silence. He hesitated to tell Cathy what was happening. He feared how she would react, as she had always leaned on Dave for strength and reassurance in that answer from God.

But one day, Cathy asked: "Dave, am I going to be all right? What does God tell you?"

Not wanting to meet her eye, Dave finally responded. God wasn't providing the usual answer. In the silence, Dave believed the answer was that Cathy would not recover from her cancer—at least, she would not recover physically.

Dave braced himself for Cathy's tears. Looking up to meet her eyes, however, it wasn't tears Dave saw. Instead, he saw a face full of peace and acceptance.

"I'm not going to make any deals with God," Cathy said finally. "I told Him all along that I wanted to live long enough to see Amy get married, and Brent and David graduate from high school. But I'll be ready when He is."

David's graduation was three months away. He was living in Battle Creek, Michigan, which allowed him to pursue his dream of playing hockey. However, he would be graduating from Boyne City High School on Memorial Day weekend. He'd been reluctant to go so far from home due to his mother's health, but Cathy insisted he take what was right for him.

When Dave and Cathy were absent Sundays, we knew they were downstate watching David play hockey. The route on U.S. 131 South always took them over the "love tunnel."

For years, Dave and Cathy had joked about a major culvert at mile marker 147. Someday, they'd said for years as they sped over the ten-foot-tall culvert, they were going to pull off the road and make out in their "love tunnel." Of course, they never had because they were in a hurry, or because they just realized it was a silly, teen-age kind of idea.

One day on their way to see David play hockey, however, Dave pulled the car off the road. "What are you doing?" Cathy started to ask. Then she realized they were directly above their "love tunnel."

Dave came around the vehicle and helped Cathy from her seat, and then held her as they walked down the hill and into the culvert. There, they kissed—a far cry from the "make-out" session they envisioned all those years. But as they returned hand-in-hand to their car, Dave realized he had just made a memory for every future journey down U.S. 131.

On March 2, Cathy and Dave celebrated their twenty-fifth anniversary. For the event, Amy, Eric, Brent and David reserved a room for their parents at the Grand Traverse Resort in Traverse City. Dave and Cathy went to the luxury hotel and spent the night making love and celebrating their life. They were both aware Cathy's strength was fading, but the cancer was not going to deny them one more chance to show their passion for one another.

By this time, my responsibilities as a pastor had been extended to a second church: Greensky Hill United Methodist Church. The log cabin church was more than 150 years old, and had been started as a Native American mission church. The thirty-some members continued to include Ojibway in the weekly worship as they prayed the Lord's Prayer and sang at least one hymn in their native language.

Horton Bay had been a little reluctant to share their pastor, but Cathy had been instrumental in gaining support. "I realize I'm just being selfish," she admitted in one meeting. "I still want Pastor Kathy to have lunch with me, and be here on Sunday mornings and Wednesday evenings. And then I realized, she can do that and have people from Greensky join us for lunch, have her for worship, and have extra services, too."

With Cathy's encouragement, Horton Bay United Methodist Church approved of the two-point charge. We soon felt like we'd always been one parish.

As Easter approached, I particularly wanted a special symbol of our union in Christ. For what I had in mind, I needed Dave's help. When I explained what I needed, Dave took some cedar wood he had behind his home. He stripped off the bark and fashioned a cross, and then drilled holes in two parallel rows the length and width of the cross.

On Maundy Thursday, the cross was positioned in a Christmas tree stand in front of the pews at Horton Bay. Members of Horton Bay and Greensky Hill shared communion as we remembered Jesus and His disciples in the Last Supper.

I then provided nails to the congregation. The nails, I said, represented our sins—sins that ultimately had nailed Jesus to the cross. "I know some of you want to hide the nail in your purse or pocket, and carry it out of here," I said. "But don't you see—this is the very reason Jesus went to the cross. You can't eliminate your sin, but Jesus can—if you give it to Him."

One by one, parishioners came forward and hammered the heavy black nails into the cross. The mood in the darkened sanctuary was somber and meditative as we sang our last hymn.

Three days later, on April 12, people began congregating at Greensky Hill at 6:30 A.M. Northern Michigan isn't known for early springs, but that year, the morning dawned warm enough for an outdoors sunrise service. We arranged a few pews in the grassy area between the church and fellowship hall, with Dave's cross standing in front of us.

As the sun began to rise, we sang *Christ the Lord Is Risen Today*, alternating verses in English and Ojibway. I read the Easter story as depicted in John 20. Even as we heard how the Son rose that day, the sun slowly rose behind us, peaking through the trees and reflecting off Susan Lake. The smells of wet ground and new growth were in the air.

As we sang our final hymn, people came forward and placed white paper lilies into the empty nail holes of the cross. Soon, the cross was transformed from a scarred, ugly piece of wood into a creation of white-covered beauty.

"Let us pray," I said as the echo died from the final words of the hymn. I'd bowed my head but, before I could speak, the sounds of a woodpecker came from the surrounding trees.

Cathy kept shaking her head in awe when she tried to speak to me afterwards. "It was so beautiful," she said. "Just being outdoors and thinking about Jesus on that first Easter—what a way to celebrate the resurrection."

It was one of the last special events Cathy could attend. She came to the annual Mother-Daughter Supper in early May, but became overheated. Dave, who had been working in the kitchen, came to her side and escorted her home.

As soon as hockey ended, David returned home to finish his coursework at Boyne City. Days before his graduation, however, Cathy went into the hospital. She was weakening fast, and her abdomen was now noticeably distended from the tumors growing inside her.

Officials at the Boyne City Schools graciously informed the Cadarettes that although graduates were supposed to receive their diplomas in alphabetical order, David would be the first in line.

Then, even if Cathy were unable to stay for the entire ceremony, she would at least see her son graduate.

The night of graduation, I sat with Jim and Inge Ledahl in the bleachers on the east side of the gymnasium. As the graduates filed down the aisle two by two, we looked across the gym. Dave was just coming through the front doors, pushing Cathy in her wheelchair. They stopped in front of the first row of bleachers.

During the speeches and awards, Dave had to take Cathy outside a couple of times when she became overheated. She insisted as soon as she recovered, however, upon returning to their place in the bleachers.

There, Cathy sat in pride and joy as "David J. Cadarette Jr." was announced on stage, and her son walked across to receive his diploma.

As the school band played the recessional, the graduates began to leave. David, however, took a detour around the front of the folding chairs to where his mother sat. Cathy stood, and the two embraced. For what seemed liked hours, mother and son held each other tightly.

Cathy's prayers had been answered: she had seen her youngest graduate. Instead of six months, she'd lived almost four years—double the time of anyone else with mesothelioma, according to her oncologist.

God had not forgotten His promises. God's promise of eternal life now remained.

Chapter

So we do not lose heart. Even though our outer nature is wasting away, our inner nature is being renewed day by day. For this slight momentary affliction is preparing us for an eternal weight of glory beyond all measure.
—II Corinthians 4:16-17

I t was a northern Michigan sunset worthy of applause.

The blazing red sun hung low to the ground, filling the sky with pinks and purples matched only by a painter's palette. Silhouettes of tall white pine trees stood against the distant shore, and the entire scene was multiplied by two by the reflection of the waters of Little Traverse Bay.

Somewhere in the city, tourists were pulling off the road to take pictures. At an area restaurant, patrons were taking time out from their meal to applaud—a local tradition.

Through the windows of Northern Michigan Hospital, the sunset provided a needed relief from the vigil by Cathy's bedside. But as I watched the fading rays, I realized this would be the last sunset in Cathy's life.

Three nights before—a lifetime, it seemed—Dave called me at home. "Cathy is back in the hospital," he said. "The doctors say it's only a matter of time."

I immediately drove the eleven miles to the hospital and went directly to Room 277. Dave, Amy, Eric, Brent and I were gathered around Cathy's bed with plastered smiles on our faces. We had expected this moment for three and a half years. Still, we didn't quite know what to say or do.

And then David arrived. He came into the room with that same look of shock and disbelief as us, and he too tried to put on the brave front. Within a few seconds, however, his six-foot-one frame dissolved, and he laid his head on his mother's shoulder, sobs racking his frame.

The rest of us began to cry with him. All of us—except Cathy. Putting her arms around her youngest, she looked at Dave and matter-of-factly stated, "He's taking this hard, isn't he?"

That's when Dave knew Cathy was completely at rest in the Lord. Here was a woman whose first thought was her children, who so easily showed emotions through her tears. Yet here she was, almost analytically looking over the scene and being at peace with what she saw.

We prayed together, and then began to relax. Cathy's chortle joined our laughter as David confessed the police stopped him on his way to the hospital after clocking him at 105 mph. Cathy joined us in telling funny stories on one another.

As the evening continued, however, Cathy seemed to slip into a light coma. She had a morphine-drip to help with her pain, but it also was affecting her breathing. Our light-heartedness disappeared, and we gathered around Cathy's bedside. I began reading scripture: Psalm 23, John 14, and other words of comfort and hope. We also began to sing a few hymns.

After a couple of hours, however, Cathy suddenly woke up, smiled at us all and said, "OK, everyone, time to go to sleep." Then, as she snuggled down in her bed, she announced, "Good night."

We looked at each other with grins, shook our heads, and watched Cathy fell into a gentle sleep. I thought about staying the night, but I was urged by the Cadarettes to go home.

About 7 A.M. Saturday, however, the phone rang. It was Amy. "Mom needs you," she said in an urgent voice. I threw on clothes and headed back to the hospital. There, I found Cathy in a very restless mood. "Why haven't I gone?" she asked me. "I'm ready to go. Why doesn't Jesus come for me? Is there something I haven't done right?"

"God hasn't come for you yet because it must not be time," I assured her. "You might be ready, but God won't come for you until God is ready."

As Cathy fell back to sleep, Amy gave me the greatest compliment of my ministry. "Mom woke up panicked and said she couldn't see Jesus," she said. "She told us, 'Call P.K. She can always help me see Jesus.'"

Cathy drifted in and out of consciousness Saturday. She was coherent when awake, but her sleep would increasingly be deep and filled with gasps for every breath.

The family also gasped when, during one of her more lucid moments, Cathy seriously asked, "Will you forget me?" We almost in unison responded, "How could we ever forget you?"

Along with immediate family, others began congregating—Cathy's mother, Dave's parents, Jan Leist and Harold and Ruth Koteskey, friends from work and church. We continued to sing praise choruses together, pray together, and share stories about Cathy.

At one point, Dave had to pull Harold aside. "Do you remember that day you anointed Cathy?" Dave asked, as Harold nodded his head. "I distinctly remember as you prayed, you said, 'If it is not your will to provide physical healing, may Cathy have three or four good years of life left to her.' Did you know that's how long she had?"

Harold admitted he didn't remember the words he prayed, but he didn't dispute Dave's memory. "The Holy Spirit must have been whispering in my ear that day," he said.

As I prepared to leave that night, I encouraged family members to tell Cathy anything they wanted. As a hospital chaplain, I'd experienced times when people seemingly in comas would awake and recall entire conversations that took place around their beds. "The hearing seems to be the last sense to go," I told them. "Tell her whatever you want. Even if she doesn't respond to what you say, she very may well be able to hear what you're saying."

Sunday morning, I preached at Greensky Hill and told them about Cathy's condition. At Horton Bay, however, a special speaker had been scheduled. During the opening announcements, I explained I was planning to return to the hospital because I felt my place was with the Cadarette family at that moment.

"I would like to invite you to all come to the hospital after services today to pray for Cathy and her family," I said. "I've been telling the family and I'll tell you—I don't want any stiff upper lips. Saying good-bye is a hard thing to do, but it needs to be done before we can get on with the business of living."

When I arrived at the hospital, Cathy was in a deep sleep. I told the family that people from the church would be coming after services. They began picking up pizza boxes and other trash, straightening the room as if preparing for Sunday company.

A few minutes to noon, the Horton Bay family began to arrive. Soon, more than fifty people were crowding into the hospital room and spilling out into the hall. Most hugged Dave and the kids as they arrived; some spoke to Cathy without any response.

And then, Ed Williamson came into the room. Ed reminds me of Hoss Cartwright from the old TV show *Bonanza*—a giant of a man, and yet with the tender heart of a teddy bear. Coming to Cathy's side, Ed leaned over her. "Hey, Cathy," he said gently. "It's me—big Ed." Cathy opened her eyes, focused on Ed—and broke into a big smile. Ed broke down into tears.

Dave and his family gathered around the bed. The rest of those in the room joined hands, and we prayed. We thanked God for Cathy—for her witness and her spirit and what it had meant to Horton Bay church. We prayed for the family and for our church as we realized Cathy's absence would leave quite a hole in our hearts.

After the "amen," Cathy gasped out, "Lord, I'm ready! Take me now!" Her family immediately clustered around her, weeping. Cathy breathed deeply for a few minutes, but then she opened her eyes again. She looked directly at me.

I assured her: "You're not doing anything wrong," I said. "You believe in Jesus Christ as your Savior. That's all you need to do. God will come when it is time."

It was among the last words we heard from Cathy. Through the rest of the afternoon, she slept continuously, her breathing becoming more labored. Dave wouldn't leave her side, not even for meals. "You want me here, don't you," he'd ask Cathy. We had to admit her breathing, even as she slept, changed a little as if in agreement.

By Monday morning, Cathy was comatose, with no sign of recognizing anyone present. Brent asked that I anoint Cathy with oil, as Harold had anointed her almost four years ago. I hadn't brought any oil with me, but rummaging through a drawer, we found some hand cream.

Placing a dab in my hand, I leaned over Cathy's sleeping form. I told her how much she meant to us all, and how we would one day be with her again in heaven because of the grace of Jesus Christ. I then drew a cross on Cathy's forehead, ending my prayer with "In the name of the Father, the Son and Holy Spirit, amen."

Then, I felt the Holy Spirit speak to me. "Don't stop there," the Spirit whispered. "There are others in this room who will need healing in the days and weeks ahead. Anoint everyone in this room."

This wasn't anything they taught in seminary. However, I believed the direction was from God. Turning to the Dave, I made the sign of the cross on his head with the hand cream. One by one, I walked around the room, and marked a cross on each person's forehead. When I had finished, I stopped before the last person and ask that they mark me with the oil.

Sometime that day, Cathy's linen needed to be changed. Dave picked up his wife and held her as the nurses changed the bedding. Dave himself changed her gown without any sense of revulsion or embarrassment.

Towards sundown, I started to say my good-byes, when Jan Leist stopped me. "Don't go just yet," she said, looking at Cathy. I then realized Cathy's breathing had changed.

We called the nurses. One of them came in and checked Cathy's vital signs, then said to Dave quietly, "If there's anyone who isn't here, you should call them right away."

Once again, Dave had to call his youngest son, David. It took almost thirty minutes for David to join us. During that time, we weren't sure whether Cathy would make it.

However, almost as soon as David walked through the door, Cathy rallied. I wasn't sure if God wasn't ready for Cathy, or if Cathy was determined not to die in David's presence. Either way, the nurse just shook her head. "I can't believe it, but I think she's going to make it through another night," she told Dave.

With Dave's assurance that he would call if there were any change, I kissed Cathy's cheek, and walked down the hall. Stopping in the visitor's lounge, I found Jan Leist. With her, I gazed out at the glorious sunset until the light completely faded. "I have to work tomorrow, but you'll call me if there's any change, won't you," asked Jan in a thoughtful tone of voice.

I assured her I would. I admired the view for a few more minutes, and then headed out of the hospital—praying for strength for whatever the next day would bring.

Chapter

God will wipe every tear from their eyes. Death will
be no more; mourning and crying and pain will be no
more, for the first things have passed away.
—Revelation 21:4

D ave was losing track of the days.

He'd come into the hospital Friday afternoon, and hadn't left Cathy's room for more than a couple of minutes. Only by checking the date on his watch could he believe it was Tuesday, June 16, 1998.

Dave was noticeably thinner—not so much from the last five days, but the last five months. His face also was a little blotched, with patches of dried skin. "My medication is at home," he said. "If I go without it for a few days, my skin starts to flake."

That's why, when I entered Cathy's room Tuesday morning, I found the fewest number of people I'd seen in five days. Only Amy, Eric and Brent sat with Dave and Cathy. David had gone to lift weights—a way to relieve some of the stress from the past few days. Cathy's mother had returned to her home in Alpena. Dave's parents had gone to Dave's home for a breather, and to pick up Dave's medication and some clean clothes.

A rattle accompanied every breath Cathy took. The family had alerted the nurse's desk, asking that Cathy's airway be cleared of mucus.

Unlike previous days, Cathy wasn't the focus of our attention. Dave, the kids and I chatted about everyday matters. I considered asking Dave about funeral arrangements, but didn't feel right doing so in Cathy's presence. And something kept telling me Dave wasn't ready.

Around lunchtime, Judy Caldecott walked into the room. Judy was head of the Horton Bay Sunday School program, and my cross-country skiing buddy. As we were clustered in a group away from Cathy's bed, we discussed whether Judy and I should get lunch for the group or we should go as a group to the hospital cafeteria. "You could use a few minutes outside this room," I said to Dave.

Dave hesitated for a second, and I thought he was going to agree with us. Then he glanced over at Cathy in her bed. A single teardrop was rolling down her cheek.

"Hey, what are you crying about," he asked in a kidding voice, heading over to her. Then he stopped. Cathy had stopped breathing.

Amy immediately dashed into the hall and yelled for a nurse. The rest of us came around the bed, but we knew Cathy was gone. Heavy, bloody mucus was coming from her mouth.

"Oh, Lord, not like this," I whispered in anguish as Dave, Amy, Eric and Brent came to Cathy's side. I had seen others go peacefully in their last minutes. There wasn't any peace as the nurse rushed into the room, and tried to put an instrument down Cathy's throat to clear it.

After a few efforts, the nurse looked up at us. She didn't need to tell us that it was over.

With their heads on Cathy's bed, Dave, Brent, Amy and Eric let their tears go. I turned to Judy, and we cried on each other's shoulders. After a few minutes, I moved behind Dave, laid a hand on his back and a hand on Cathy's arm. The others joined hands in a circle, and I began to pray.

I realized I wasn't being very professional in the moment as the words faltered out. But at the moment, I didn't feel like a pastor. I felt like "P.K.," and I'd just lost a friend.

As we lifted our heads, we saw Dick Rickard standing back by the door. Dick, also a member of Horton Bay, had attended many of the Promise Keepers' events with Dave. He had been driving through Petoskey on his way to a job, but something told him to stop at the hospital.

He embraced Dave, and the two wept for a few minutes. Then Dave began to compose himself, thinking of all the people he needed to call.

Nurses came in to clean Cathy up, so we moved to the other side of the room to make the phone calls. The first one was to David Jr. I could hear the anguish in Dave's voice as he tried to comfort his son over the phone.

Then, Dave was ready to discuss funeral arrangements. "I don't want any visitation," he said. "Cathy's father died when she was sixteen, and all she could remember was him lying in the casket. She didn't want that to be her kids' memory of her."

Cathy had indicated she'd liked to be cremated, and Dave wanted to dump her ashes in Horton Creek behind their house. However, he wanted a memorial service at Horton Bay church.

"Sometimes, when a service takes place at a church, it's hard for family to go back to that place," I cautioned Dave. "The memory they have is of the service, although this is more true when there's a casket present in the sanctuary."

Dave didn't hesitate. "No, it's right that it takes place at Horton Bay," he said. "That was Cathy's church—that's where we should have the memorial."

Judy was Horton Bay's coordinator for funeral dinners, so she immediately set out on her job to call volunteers to provide dinner after the service. Dick, known for some of the tightest bear hugs in all of Horton Bay, embraced Dave one more time, and headed back to work.

Brent, Amy and Eric were ready to go, but Dave wanted to wait for one more person: Dr. A.J. D'Errico, Cathy's oncologist. For almost four years, this caring doctor had marveled at Cathy's progress. When Dave learned the doctor was on his way to the room, he waited.

Dr. D'Errico soon arrived. He was very quiet as he placed his stethoscope to Cathy's chest. After a couple of moments, he pronounced the time of her death.

Dave hugged the doctor and thanked him for all of his service. Dr. D'Errico, in his silence, made it clear he too had just lost a special person—someone who had become more than a patient; someone he too would miss.

We then prepared to leave the room. Because there would be no viewing, Dave realized this would be his last time to see his wife's mortal remains. The rest of us waited in the hallway, allowing him privacy as he returned to say good-bye to Cathy.

I hugged the family members in the hallway, and then headed to my car in a separate parking lot. Once I reached the solitude of my car, I really let my tears go. "Oh, Lord, I just wish it could have been any other way," I sobbed, leaning over the steering wheel.

The vigil of the past four days overwhelmed me. Cathy was gone—really gone. No more singing TV theme songs with me. No more cappuccino breaks with Jan. No more yelling encouragement at David's hockey games. No more fishing with Brent. No more daily phone conversations with Amy. No more holding Dave's hand.

But also, no more pain. No more chemo. No more radiation. No more worrying about what awaited her at the end of her physical journey.

I thought of all the times these past few days that Room 277 had been full of people. So many times, those persons were in tears at Cathy's bedside.

How appropriate, I thought, that at the moment of her death, and her new life, the last vision Cathy had was Dave with just a few family members and friends nearby to support him. We hadn't been gathered in sorrow at her bedside; we were gathered around one another, laughing and planning—and living.

It had to have been a vision that confirmed her hope and gave her the strength to say good-bye to this life. Even as she clasped Jesus' hand to be welcomed to new life, Cathy had offered her final good-bye to us—a single tear. Tears had always been Cathy's way of expressing sorrow. They also, however, had been shared whenever Cathy offered praises of immeasurable joy and love.

"Thank you, Lord," I prayed and, drying my eyes, I started the car engine to head home.

Chapter 14

Jesus said to Martha, "I am the resurrection and the life. Those who believe in me, even though they die, will live, and everyone who lives and believes in me will never die. Do you believe this?"
—John 11:25-26

The sanctuary at Horton Bay comfortably seats 100 people. On Easter and Christmas, we add rows of chairs to the aisles and back walls, and squeeze in 150.

For Cathy's memorial service, more than 220 people filled the sanctuary and overflowed into the Education Wing. Most of them, as they shook my hand or gave me a hug, whispered in my ear, "I'm glad I'm not in your shoes."

As my eyes scanned the crowd, the painfully shy public speaker in me wished I weren't in my shoes, either. But I kept recalling the words of a seminary professor: "If we as Christians have nothing to say in the face of death, then we have nothing to say, period." And I knew a lot needed to be said about Cathy's death.

That Friday, as I stepped up to the pulpit to start Cathy's memorial service, I walked by dozens of floral arrangements lining the altar rail. A table was filled with Cathy's pictures and beloved knickknacks, including her brown and white checkerboard box of folded Kleenex.

"Friends, we have gathered here to praise God and to witness to our faith as we celebrate the life and new life of Cathy Cadarette,"

I began. "We come together in grief, acknowledging our human loss. May God grant us grace, that in pain we may find comfort, in sorrow hope, in death resurrection."

After reading a eulogy, I invited people to share their memories. Ordinarily, two or three relatives or friends will respond with a story or two. For Cathy, fifteen people came forward.

I'd been holding back my tears, trying to be "professional." All my resolve broke, however, when I saw Amy, Brent and David Jr. stand up together and come to a microphone to share a few simple words of love about their mom. As they finished, Brent added, "In my eyes, she beat the cancer."

The last person to speak was Dave. "I took some paper to bed with me last night to write down what I was going to say," he confessed. "But I fell asleep. I awoke in the middle of the night and talked to God for a while, but still didn't feel any particular words were given to me. So, I'm just going to shoot from the hip."

He began as he always did, praising God. Dave noted that he and Cathy didn't get to Sunday school or church as often as they could have. They didn't know everything about the Bible and church. But, Dave finished, "The Lord doesn't want people who know everything. The Lord wants people who will give Him their whole hearts. That's what Cathy did."

As the service continued, the people read Psalm 23 in unison, and then Ed Chamberlain read John 11:17-44, the story of Jesus raising Lazarus from the dead.

As I arose to give the funeral message, I felt an incredible sense of God's presence and peace. I knew it was time for this Christian to say something in the face of death.

"One of the last mornings Cathy was in the hospital, she became very restless," I told the mourners. "As we watched, she lifted her left hand and reached over to her right wrist. Her fingers touched the plastic hospital bracelet and moved on. They touched the plastic allergy bracelet and moved on. Cathy then felt the cloth WWJD bracelet on her wrist, and hooked her finger into it until she calmed down again.

"WWJD—what would Jesus do? We don't always know what Jesus would do because we don't always have scripture to help us know. But we do know what Jesus would do in response to the death of a friend, for we are told what Jesus did when his friend Lazarus died."

I reminded the congregation how, when Jesus first arrived at the sisters' home, Martha said to him, "Lord, if you had been here, my brother would not have died." How many of us, I asked, have been saying to God this week, "Lord, if you had only been here, Cathy would not have died."

But then I reminded them that Jesus was as present alongside Cathy's bedside as he had been at the tomb of his friend Lazarus. And when Jesus arrived at the tomb, His first response was to weep. "Jesus wept," I said. "Even knowing what heaven was like, Jesus wept. Even knowing that in a few seconds, Lazarus would stand before them again, Jesus wept.

"Jesus wept because He saw the power that death had on the friends and family. And being human, Jesus wept because He too felt loss.

"We too must weep today. I hope most of us here know Cathy is in heaven this day. I believe all of us are assured Cathy is better off today, for her pain and suffering have ended. And yet, we too must weep, because we feel the physical loss today."

I explained to visitors that Cathy was the one who taught us we had to let our tears out. She sometimes worried her tears would be interpreted as a sign of weakness. But we assured her, "Cathy, your tears are a gift to us, because they are an honest emotion. It helps us celebrate who you are."

Don't think that our tears at Cathy's death meant our faith was weak, I emphasized. Tears bring healing. They are like a dam used to regulate the water. If too much water is held in, the pressure builds up until something has to crack inside. But if the water is released a little at a time—if tears are allowed to fall a few at a time—then pressure and grief are released.

The other question I felt I had to deal with at Cathy's memorial was why God didn't choose to heal Cathy the way He did Lazarus. "But consider," I said, "we would not find a 2000-year-old man named Lazarus still walking this earth today. The point of the miracle was *not* that Lazarus would never die. The point of the miracle was to allow Jesus to show the people what resurrection would look like. They all would die, even Lazarus. However, new life would come as a result."

God created all of this earth, and pronounced every part of it good, I said. Humans, on the other hand, created asbestos products—humans with limited understanding and compassion. God did not will Cathy to get cancer from exposure to asbestos, but when she got it, God intervened.

"In October 1994, Cathy went into a tomb of despair, of fear, of hurt, of sorrow," I said. "Then God called, 'Cathy, come forth,' and Cathy came out of her tomb into new life as a creature who believed in God, with a husband who believed in God. She came out into a new life of grace."

Somewhere in the congregation, I heard a gasp. On others faces, I saw a new light of understanding, so I continued:

"In 1995, as Cathy underwent her first chemo treatments, she started back into that tomb. But Jesus called, 'Cathy, come forth,' and she came out of her tomb into the joy of seeing Brent graduate from high school.

"In 1996, Cathy slipped back into her tomb when she learned she needed surgery and radiation for breast cancer. But Jesus called, 'Cathy, come forth,' and she came out of her tomb into new life as a mother-in-law as Amy and Eric were married.

"This past Memorial Day weekend, we thought we'd lost Cathy. But Jesus said, 'Cathy, come forth,' and Cathy came out to see David's new life as he graduated from high school.

"Last Tuesday, for the last time, God called, 'Cathy, come out,' and Cathy's spirit left that cancer-ridden tomb, and went to be with Jesus in a new life of joy and peace."

God healed Cathy, I said. Maybe the healing wasn't the form we would have preferred, but God took away the pain of her imperfect body to give her a new perfect body—one that we each through the grace of Jesus would see again one day.

"In the name of the Father, Son and Holy Spirit, amen," I concluded.

As I turned to our final hymn, I thought how often Cathy would ask me to get something down to the nuts and bolts. I had to smile as I thought, "Well, that was definitely a Cathy sermon."

Chapter 15

God leads me beside still waters; He restores my soul.
—Psalm 23:2

Surely King David knew of Horton Creek when he wrote about still waters in Psalm 23.

The small creek on the west side of Horton Bay comes alive when a brook trout fights the fishing line. Otherwise, little disturbs the peace of the creek or its surroundings.

This is especially true near a footbridge owned by Dave and Jeannie Babbitt. People don't disturb it, as it is only accessible by foot and on private land. The area also is downhill a little, giving shelter from any winds.

Dave knew this was the place to scatter Cathy's ashes. He asked the Babbitts' permission, and they agreed. Two days after Cathy's memorial—after attending Sunday services at Horton Bay—Dave, Amy, Eric, Brent and David went to the bridge with the container of Cathy's ashes.

At Cathy's memorial, the sanctuary had overflowed with people. At the outdoor sanctuary built by God, however, only five gathered to say their farewells. Tears flowed as freely as the waters of Horton Creek as the family gathered in their memories and their grief.

Then after a prayer, Dave opened the container, and allowed Cathy's ashes to fall freely into the waters. After watching them flow away, the family returned home.

One of their first acts after arriving home Tuesday from the hospital had been to empty the medicine cabinet of every one of

Cathy's medications. Going through Cathy's clothes and personal items took more time, as each person saved an item that had special meaning to them.

Dave found Cathy's floral-covered journal, and read through the too-few pages. He also uncovered an empty journal, one whose front cover featured a cowboy on horseback in the shadows of a valley. The journal was inscribed by Brent, who gave it to his father as a Christmas present in 1995.

At the time, Dave hadn't felt like writing down his thoughts. Now, however, as evenings came and he climbed alone into a king-sized bed, he felt much like that cowboy in the shadows. He opened the journal and began writing.

I didn't realize how much you can learn about someone till you read their journal, he wrote as he reflected upon the words Cathy had left in her own journal. *Not only them, but the impact on other people including yourself.*

Cathy left us 2 weeks ago today. I sure do miss her. I miss her most when I lay down here at night and get ready to say my prayers. My first thing I pray is that I am in the Lord and He is in me, as the Bible says. I ask that Cathy being with the Lord to let our spirits pray together as we always did. I really feel close to her then.

I pray that until I can go with Cathy and kneel along side her again in your presence, that I can use the remembrance of Cathy's love and our suffering to help others to see you.

At Sunday worship services, Dave continued to stand in his pew and witness to this love experienced from God and the members. Often, he came to the altar rail to pray; seldom, however, was he left alone there, as Dick Rickard or other friends came to kneel alongside him, offering comfort and love.

Even those who didn't publicly show their support continued to ask me how Dave was doing. One weekend in particular, the parsonage phone began to ring almost every five minutes. "Did you know Dave's house is up for sale?" each anxious parishioner asked. "We saw a sign out in front of his house. Is he planning to move?"

I drove around the corner to Horton Bay Road and, sure enough, a homemade "For Sale" sign stood in front of the white, two-story farmhouse. "Oh, we're not moving," Dave reassured me. "I just figured with the extra people in town for the July 4th weekend, it was a good time to see if there was interest in buying my house."

Cathy and Dave had always planned to build a home for their retirement years further back on the property, and then to sell the farmhouse. After the weekend, with no inquiries on the house, Dave removed the sign.

Dave kept busy in his vegetable garden, a source of pride and joy in past summers. He tilled the earth, planted seeds and began the endless chore of weeding.

However, he soon realized there was a significant difference from former years. Before, he could get lost in his garden for hours, because Cathy's praise always made him forget the sweat, dirt and sore muscles. Now, the work only felt like that—work.

I went down to the garden today and realized I didn't care if it grew or not, he wrote. *I picked a blackberry and started crying. I don't even want to be here anymore.*

Every time, everyday I did stuff in the garden, Cathy was always there to tell how good it looked or something that always lifted me up. If it wasn't for my kids, I'd just die of a heartache. I know the Lord brought us a long way and I know he's taking good care of mom, but he sure has left a big, big hole. I trust in what he's got next; I just don't like this lonely time right now.

I want to fill that empty spot, but there's no one on earth could ever love me so truly, so unconditionally as Cathy did. No one but God himself.

I don't know if I'll ever remarry. Cath said she wanted me to. She didn't want me to be lonely. I will always miss her whether I fill my time with the Lord or remarry or work, for her and her love will always be with me, thanks to God.

Between the journal and strolls to "Cathy's bridge," Dave found comfort, and began the task of living again.

Chapter 16

*Now God is God not of the dead, but of the living;
for to Him all of them are alive.*
—Luke 20:38

About a week after Cathy's memorial service, Dave called me. "Brent went fishing at Ferry Beach and accidentally locked his keys in his truck," he said. "Would you like to go with me to unlock his truck?"

I had a lot of reasons to say no. I was still catching up with work that was set aside while Cathy had been in the hospital. My sermon, due in three days, was written in my head, but hadn't been transferred to paper yet.

It crossed my mind, however, that Dave really wanted to talk about his grief, and was using this invitation as a pretext. I agreed to the drive, and soon found myself seated next to Dave, heading west toward Charlevoix.

We chatted freely for a couple of minutes, and then I asked how he and the kids were doing. "Fine," he said, not taking his eyes off the road.

That was the extent of grief counseling for the day. Dave obviously wasn't ready to talk, so I didn't push the subject.

We arrived at the docks, where Brent's truck was parked, and waved to him out in the bay. Dave unlocked Brent's driver-side door, set his keys on the truck seat, and we left. (One of the joys of small-town living—being able to leave your vehicle unlocked without fear.)

On the way back through town, Dave turned left into the Dairy Queen parking lot. "What would you like?" he asked, pulling out his wallet. I knew better than to debate who should pay for the treats. I asked for a chocolate-dipped cone, and Dave soon returned to the truck with two.

We continued to make small talk as we ate our cones in the truck, and then Dave started the engine and we headed back to Horton Bay.

As Dave drove, I realized this was unusual, for me to be talking directly to Dave. Through the past four years, most of my discussions had been with Cathy, or with Cathy and Dave. I couldn't remember any time I had talked with Dave alone.

Once at home, I thanked Dave for the ice cream, and headed back inside the parsonage. Dave waved, and headed back out of my driveway. I headed back into my office, and sat down at the typewriter to work on my sermon.

However, the words didn't start flowing on the paper for my Sunday sermon. Instead, I found I was delivering a sermon in my head to myself.

While in seminary in Ohio, I attended a mandatory training session on clergy misconduct. The session was repeated when I arrived in Michigan as a new pastor. And in just a few months, another session was being mandated for all clergy in our conference.

In other words, the church was very sensitive to issues of clergy interaction with parishioners—particularly when both were single. I knew the list of do's and don'ts recommended by the church, and had followed them faithfully. Actually, it had been easy, as almost all the other single persons in my parish were women or elderly men.

But for the first time, I realized being with Dave was raising some red flags in my conscience. What if someone had seen Dave and me in his truck eating ice cream cones? How would—or maybe more importantly, could—they interpret seeing the two of us together?

Not that I had any romantic interest in Dave Cadarette. In fact, I couldn't think of any two people more opposite than Dave and me.

I knew the location of every bookstore within a three-county radius. Dave had read two books in his life.

I held a bachelor's degree and a master's degree; to my knowledge, Dave had only attended the School of Hard Knocks.

My worst subject in school had been physical education; in fact, if it weren't for dancing classes, I'd still be struggling through my last credits at college. Dave played hockey and softball, loved scuba diving and fishing, and had a perpetual tan from being active outdoors.

I was so organized, I knew which Bible text I would use three months in advance. Dave would look out the window in the morning and decide which roofing job to do that day—and might change his mind after breakfast.

Besides, I knew whoever married Dave would have big shoes to fill as his wife. Cathy had been a special lady in her own right, but Dave's sense of her perfection had been multiplied a thousand times over.

Certainly, whoever became Dave's wife would also become stepmother to his kids. Although Dave's kids were grown to the point they didn't need a "mother," whoever married their father would have to take into account their feelings.

Moreover, one measure of acceptance by the kids and Dave would be whether they felt Cathy would have approved of Dave's new wife.

A few years before, I conducted one Bible study when we were discussing the trick question posed in Luke 20:27-40. The teachers told a story of a woman who in turn married each of seven brothers. When asked which of the seven brothers would claim the woman as his wife in heaven, Jesus replied that the dead don't marry.

"You mean Dave won't be married to me in heaven?" Cathy asked during the study.

"Not exactly," I said. "Jesus is saying all of us will be related as brothers and sisters in heaven, so in fact we will all be family."

"Well, I'm not sure I like that," Cathy said. "I want Dave in my mansion up there!"

As I considered all these things, I decided I needed some direction. Turning from my typewriter to the phone, I called Judy Caldecott.

Judy was my cross-country ski buddy during the winter, but she also was my swimming buddy in the summer. I invited her to meet me the following week at Young State Park.

Actually, as arranged, we met on a side street alongside the park, using the beach just outside the park limits. The sand contains a few more stones than the park's beach, but the water feels just as good.

After a few minutes' swim, Judy and I returned to our beach blankets. I found a stick and made a tic-tac-toe graph in the sand. Judy and I were soon marking our X's and O's as we talked.

"Let me ask you something," I said. I hesitated, and added, "This is strictly between you and me."

"OK," she said, which I knew meant our private conversation would be kept private.

I told her about Dave and me going to Charlevoix the previous week. "How do you think the church would feel about the two of us having informal meetings like that?" I said.

"I mean," I quickly added, "I don't expect any kind of relation to develop here. I just figure he's alone, he's naturally going to offer more invitations like that, and those occasions might be easier for him to talk about his grief than if he came into the office for counseling. But I'm wondering how anyone from the church would feel if they saw us together alone."

Judy thought long before she answered. "I think you're going to have to be very careful and go very slow," she said. "I hadn't thought about it, but it would be tricky, trying to counsel him as pastor and yet not being alone with him."

"The church has told us to never counsel anyone alone," I responded. "If Dave ever calls and needs counseling, would you mind coming to the church and just being on the premises while he's in the office with me? I'm not saying I fear anything from him—it's just that everyone has to be so careful these days."

Judy agreed she'd be available, and we went back to our tic-tac-toe and quiet conversation.

At the end of the week, Dave called. This time, he was on his way to lunch, and wondered if I'd like to join him. I politely thanked him, but said I had other work to do. We chatted for a couple of seconds, and ended the conversation.

Dave didn't call again to invite me to dinner. For a couple of months, we saw each other at services on Sunday and in the evening services, but we had no more one-on-one talks.

Until September, that is, when Dave wanted to talk to me about the new woman in his life.

Chapter

Now faith is the assurance of things hoped for,
the conviction of things not seen.

—Hebrews 11:1

True to her word, Judy Caldecott came to the church and busied herself straightening books in the library as Dave arrived for his counseling appointment with me.

As he always did when he walked through the church doors, Dave's first action was to remove his cap. He took a seat in one of the brownish folding chairs in my office as I settled into my office chair. Dave balanced his hat on his knee, and finally made eye contact with me.

"I'm seeing another woman," he said.

I realized I wasn't surprised. Having been married twenty-five years, Dave would naturally seek companionship again. And I was pleased to hear Dave felt this new woman was just his type: blond, long-legged and very beautiful.

I was surprised, however, when he went on to tell me this new woman was just a couple of years older than Amy. Maybe that's why my first question was, "How do your kids feel about your relationship?"

"OK," Dave said. "They want me to be happy."

However, Dave didn't sound happy as he spoke of this new relationship. His voice didn't have its usual strong, confident timbre. I hadn't pushed him in June to tell me how he was feeling about Cathy's death, but I did now.

"I feel like there's a hole inside me," Dave admitted. "I thought I was doing OK when she first died. But it's not getting easier; if anything, it's getting harder."

"That's to be expected," I assured him. "Immediately after Cathy died, you were surrounded by family and friends. You were kept busy with all the details surrounding Cathy's death. The death of a loved one doesn't become 'real' until a month or two after it happens. I thought it would start hitting you about now."

Dave then told me Cathy had encouraged him, in her last days, to marry again. At the time, it hadn't seemed right to him; now, he had to admit he was glad to be seeing another woman. "But has enough time passed for me to date, P.K?" he asked.

I almost grinned. I thought of the dance scene from *Gone from the Wind* when Scarlett O'Hara, confined to the black dress of a woman in mourning, couldn't keep her feet from tapping a jig under the table. Somehow, I could see Dave, trying to do the "right" thing at the expense of denying how he really felt.

"You're the only one who can answer that," I assured him. "Society used to say you must mourn for a year. Employers now tell you to mourn for a week, then get back to work. I suspect mourning is somewhere between those two periods.

"But in one sense, you've been mourning for four years," I added. "Your grief began when you first heard the prognosis for Cathy. Emotionally, you've been preparing for her death a lot longer than if she had died overnight in an accident."

Even though his dating women showed a healthy sense of getting back to life, I cautioned Dave of one danger: trying to use this new relationship as a means to escape from his grief. It was one thing to date a woman he loved; it was another to date a woman as a way to preoccupy him from thoughts of the woman he loved.

Dave didn't comment. We prayed together, and then Dave took his cap and stood up. He thanked me, and headed back out to his vehicle.

Back at home, Dave wrote in his journal, *I'm kind of getting used to crying every day. I talked to Pastor Kathy and she said I was normal and right on track, feeling the way I do. Ten years ago if anybody told me I would miss Mom the way I do, I surely wouldn't have believed them. I hope someday I will get on with it and find someone at least close to being a loving wife and Mom as Cath.*

Meanwhile at the church, Judy finished with the library and left to return home. I returned to my office, thinking not of Dave, but of Cathy.

Cathy's death was becoming real not only to Dave, but to me, too. I'd caught myself in town a couple of times waving at Cathy, only to remember that the short-haired woman getting out of the Ford Taurus couldn't be her.

I was missing Cathy's sense of joy and spunk, and her honest assessment of my sermons. At this particular moment, however, I especially missed the ability she seemed to have to get Dave to talk about himself. Whether in private meetings or at Bible studies, Cathy seemed to have the knack to get Dave to speak his thoughts out loud—a task I was finding difficult.

I prayed for continued comfort for all those who were feeling grief for Cathy, for peace and purpose in Dave's new relationship, and returned to work.

Chapter

The light shines in the darkness,
and the darkness did not overcome it.
—John 1:5

On the surface, September 1998 seemed to follow the usual pattern of life.

Leaves began changing from hues of green to a full array of red, orange and yellow. The stores were devoid of teenagers, who had returned to school, and tourists, who had returned home.

Which meant, best of all, no one honked their horns at motorists for failing to notice a traffic signal turn green. The big-city visitors had left northern Michigan, and the slower pace of living had returned until the following Memorial Day.

On the surface, too, life in the Cadarette household seemed to fall into the usual pattern of life. The basement shelves were filled with freshly canned vegetables and fruits from the garden. Amy and Eric alone canned forty-nine quarts of peaches, and Dave's parents pitched in to can tomatoes and other vegetables.

Amy celebrated her birthday. As with Brent's birthday the previous month, the family gathered around the usual birthday cake and presents. And yet, emptiness prevailed over their gathering and in their hearts as they realized they missed Cathy leading the singing of *Happy Birthday to You.*

Dave traveled with David to Grand Rapids as the latter entered trials for the Grizzlies, a Junior B hockey team. After try-outs, Dave waited until David came out of the locker room. As soon as he saw his son's face, Dave knew—his youngest was on the team. David moved to Grand Rapids to begin practices, and enrolled in classes at Grand Rapids Community College, leaving Dave's home just a little emptier.

Dave's life also felt empty. His weekend trips to watch David skate began to interfere with his participation in church services at Horton Bay. Even when he was in town, he didn't attend services or Bible study as faithfully.

Dave's work began to suffer, too. Dave had always been a Type B personality, setting his own hours and schedule. His plans were subject to change due to the weather, or a burning desire to go fishing.

Even by his usual standards, however, Dave's work began to back up. He bid jobs, but didn't feel motivated to finish them.

Dave also began frequenting the local bars. While in Alpena, Dave and his brother had owned the M-32 Club. There, Dave was a heavy drinker to accommodate all the patrons buying him a shot. Since joining Horton Bay church, Dave had become a social drinker, enjoying an occasional glass of beer with friends. Now, however, he began coming home sick from drinking too much.

Dave continued to see the woman he told me about in July. However, he also went out a few times with another, older woman. One weekend, Dave traveled to Muskegon with her to help her investigate whether to buy a home there.

While eating lunch together, she began to talk about her kids and how they were reaching the age that they didn't want to be seen with Mom. Looking up at Dave, she noticed him staring at the table. "What are you thinking about?" she asked.

"I was thinking how when our kids were gone, how much me and Cathy still had each other and how close we were getting to each other the last few years," he said. "I hope your kids take time for your loved ones and realize the money, the cars, the boats, the four-wheelers or anything else isn't worth the time you have with those you love."

After the weekend, Dave realized this wasn't the woman he wanted to spend his life with. He returned to the younger woman, with whom he began a physical relationship. In mid September, Dave spent Saturday night with her, and then headed to church on Sunday.

As he sat there, feeling that awful hole in his heart, Dave realized something. He had just spent the night with the most beautiful, the most blond, the youngest woman he could ever imagine finding. And in return, he felt nothing—he felt empty and lonely.

His family wasn't filling him. Alcohol wasn't filling him. Nothing was filling that hole left in his life by the loss of Cathy.

Or rather, he realized as he bowed his head in the pew, Dave felt like he had lost God. Somehow in trying to fill that emptiness in his life in those past few months, Dave had lost that close relationship he'd had with the thing that had mattered most in his life—even when Cathy had been alive.

When prayer time came in our services, Dave left his pew and headed to the wooden altar rail in the front of the sanctuary. He and Cathy had knelt there numerous times together. Now, he knelt without another person, but he was not alone—he knelt there with God.

"I want to get back to my first relationship with you," Dave prayed to his Lord. "I don't care if I lose this woman; I don't care if I never date another woman, or even have any desire for another woman. But God, I don't ever want to lose you."

And in that moment, Dave felt God flood his soul. God hadn't forgotten Dave, even though Dave had tried to forget God. In remembering what was most important in his life, Dave felt the black hole in his heart was filled with love—God's love for Dave.

In the following weeks, Dave continued to attend David's Saturday night hockey games, but he made every effort to get home in time for Sunday services. And on Sunday and Wednesday nights, Dave sat in the front pew, directly in front of me.

In his journal, Dave wrote, *All the time before when I didn't want to face the pain, it didn't get any better. I guess this is one of those things the Lord wanted me to learn, maybe to help others later.*

I just hope it didn't make Mom feel too bad, seeing me go through all that hurt. I don't know, but the praying sure helps. God really answers.

I asked God to help and that I was willing to accept whatever He had in store for me, not just now but forever, and He healed my heart. It's not that I don't miss Mom anymore, but that bad hurt is gone.

Chapter

> *But as it is written, "What no eye has seen, nor ear heard, nor the human heart conceived, what God has prepared for those who love him."*
> —I Corinthians 2:9

B ack home again, in Indiana, la la la, la la la la…."
I don't know all the lyrics, but I belt out those opening words every time my car crosses the state line from Michigan into the Hoosier state. In October 1997, I was especially glad to sing the words as I headed south for a one-week, fun-filled vacation in Greenfield, Indiana.

Greenfield may not be featured each week on the Travel Channel—OK, maybe it has *never* been featured on the Travel Channel or on any list of Top Ten getaways. However, it had a special attraction for me: family.

For a week, my first name wouldn't be "pastor." I had plans to do nothing except immerse myself in family and friends. My parish would be a memory until I had my fill of Hoosier hospitality.

As good as it felt to take a break, I found myself thinking about the parish during much of the eight-hour solo drive. And part of my ruminations included Dave.

Dave hadn't told me anything about his experiences in September. I had noticed he'd begun attending services faithfully again, including Wednesday evening Bible study. He'd seemed more at peace in the past month.

He'd also attended a gathering of about twenty-five singles from our parish—and seemed delighted that he was the only male. After dinner, some of the group broke into quartets to play miniature golf. Dave was quite chagrined when I beat him, especially as I was golfing with a purse over my shoulder.

"You're putting with your left hand now!" he said with surprise at one point, as I switched the putter to my left hand for a better alignment to the hole.

"Doesn't everyone?" I asked. I tried not to grin at his expression of dismay as I easily knocked the ball into the hole.

Dave soon had his revenge. As we were playing video games, Dave caught sight of me riding a mock motorcycle in front of a video screen. He tracked down Leslie Van De Car who had brought her camera to the gathering. Intent on making it to the end of the motorcycle course, I didn't realize Leslie was taking a picture of me until I heard the camera snap behind me.

For weeks afterward, before each evening service began, Dave would pull out the picture of me astraddle the motorcycle, and ask the group, "Would anyone like to see a picture of P.K.?"

The day before my vacation, the parish treated me to a surprise potluck dinner as part of Pastor Appreciation Month. My Uncle Frank and Aunt Juanita Slaughter happened to be visiting me that weekend, so they came to the dinner.

As I sat down with Frank and Juanita, I noticed Dave hovering behind me, with that boyish grin on his face and a twinkle in his blue eyes. I was glad to see the old mischievous streak in him— except when he slipped a small piece of ice down my back.

A few people gave me gifts—small items like books. As the dinner ended and people began folding up chairs, Dave took me aside to present me with his gift.

"Didn't you already give me a gift?" I asked, referring to a bag of Skittles I had found on my desk. The note said the candy was to spoil me a little for Pastor Appreciation Month, and was simply signed "Me." However, Dave was one of the few who knew my passion for Skittles (except for the green ones).

"Well, this is in addition to the Skittles," Dave said. Opening his hand, he showed me a pewter cross with the WWJD initials. "This belonged to Cathy," Dave said. "I thought it was appropriate for you to have it in her memory, considering all you did for her as her pastor."

Back at the parsonage, I showed Frank and Juanita the gifts I'd received, including Cathy's cross. I told them all about Cathy, and added that I was very touched by the fact that Dave would give me something that had belonged to her.

What I didn't admit until the ride home the next day, however, was a sense in the pit of my stomach. I had to admit I was growing uncomfortable with Dave's attention to me. The gifts from others showed appreciation for me as a pastor. Dave seemed to be stepping beyond appreciation toward affection—and into that red-flag area of pastor-parishioner relationships.

As I pulled into my parents' driveway, I knew I'd have to meet with Dave when I returned north and discuss the appropriateness of his gifts and attention. But the sight of my parents coming out to greet me washed away any more work-related thoughts. Dad gave his little girl the usual big hug of welcome; Mom began her usual fuss of showing me all the new things around their home and making sure I was settled into my old bedroom.

For three days, Horton Bay didn't enter my mind. I ate two helpings of Mom's lasagna; I giggled with my sister, Shannon, and visited with my brother, Kevin, and his family; I ran errands with Dad; I got caught up on movies.

On Thursday, we were preparing to leave the house to visit my Aunt Norma when the doorbell rang. Dad came back into the kitchen carrying a vase. A dozen red roses spilled out the top, filling the air with their pungent aroma. "They're for you," Dad said to me.

I'd only received a dozen roses twice in my life: pink ones when I turned sixteen, and red ones when I'd been working as a reporter in Frankfort, Indiana. Both times, the roses were from guys I was dating; neither time did they cement a relationship.

With some curiosity, I pulled the card off the plastic prongs and read: *Hope this finds you well. I pray the Lord blesses you with love, rest, peace. You are truly missed and you can still be spoiled long distance. With love, Me.*

"Who's 'me'"? Mom asked. "Is that Vera Hallman?"

"Uh, no," I said, trying to hide my red face among the roses. "It's Dave Cadarette. At least, that's how he signed another note to me recently."

I set the flowers on my parents' fireplace hearth, and then Dad, Mom and I climbed in their van to head to Aunt Norma's for a visit.

As we wound our way on the Old Fortville Pike—the only windy road in all of Hancock County—I was deep in thought. My suspicions that I would have to talk with Dave were now a certainty. Red roses and "with love" hinted that he was interested in me beyond being his pastor.

As I considered what I would have to say to Dave, I suddenly noticed it was quiet in the van. *Too* quiet. Silence in the presence of my mom was as rare as a quiet moment on the floor of the Wall Street Stock Exchange. Mom and Dad usually would chat with each other, if not to me. Not a peep had come from either since I'd told them who had sent the flowers.

"Uh, I was just thinking on the way down here that I was going to need to talk to Dave," I said, clearing my throat as I began. "He's been giving me other small gifts lately, and I've been thinking that we need to talk about what was appropriate."

"Absolutely," my mom immediately chimed in. She went on to recite all the things she had learned as an officer in Eden United Methodist Church, my home church. Mom had attended a few clergy misconduct seminars, too. She knew the need for pastors to set clear boundaries with their parishioners. And she knew even a hint of indiscretion could be as damaging to a congregation as actual misconduct.

"Actually," I said, "the day I return to work, I have a meeting scheduled with the district superintendent, Denny Buwalda. I'm sure he can give me some ideas as to how to handle Dave."

Assured their daughter still had a good head on her shoulders, Mom and Dad began chatting on a totally different topic. I settled back into vacation mode, and allowed myself to shut off thoughts of business once again.

I would have to talk to Dave. But it could wait at least until a few more days—time enough for another helping or two of Mom's lasagna.

Chapter 20

But speaking the truth in love, we must grow up in
every way into him who is the head, into Christ.
—Ephesians 4:15

When I met with the Rev. Denny Buwalda, he indeed had some advice for me—not only as my supervisor, but also as a friend.

"Trust those inner feelings," he said. "If you're uncomfortable, then there is more going on than simple appreciation.

"You need to talk with Dave, but be sure to invite a third person to your meeting," he added. "For one thing, it gives each of you an impartial witness to help you sort through what was said. But also, it provides some accountability to Dave for his subsequent actions."

I immediately knew the person to ask: Vera Hallman, the woman who had supplied Cathy with her Kleenex.

Vera was the first parishioner I had met outside of the church officers. She'd been copying the weekly bulletin when I'd walked into the church office. To my surprise, as soon as I introduced myself, Vera embraced me with all her might.

I later learned Vera was a native of Indiana. As a fellow ex-Hoosier, Vera delighted in telling me when my drawl would make "wash" sound like "worsh."

Although Vera was in her late sixties, the differences in our ages seemed immaterial. As she was a widow, she too knew what it was like to eat alone. We soon became lunch partners, going out to eat a couple of times each week and almost every Sunday.

Vera had one other advantage: She had known the Cadarettes long before she met me. Her old property butted up against theirs, and she'd met Brent one day when he came strolling out of the woods, looking for a lost dog.

She soon became friends with the entire family and often supplied them with her homemade vegetable soup and cornbread. I felt Dave would trust her and feel he could speak openly in front of her.

Before I could call her, however, Dave showed up at the parsonage with another twelve red roses. "I figured you couldn't bring the others from your folks' home without spilling the water," he explained to a gape-mouthed me, "so I thought you should have the benefit of another dozen."

"Been meaning to talk to you about that," I said, finally getting my mouth to work, and figuring I finally had an ideal opening to arrange a meeting with him. "Could you meet me and Vera at her condo next week?"

So it was that Vera, Dave and I settled into Vera's living room the following week in Boyne City. Vera's instructions had been to keep her mouth shut and her ears open, so she let me broach the subject of why we had come together.

"You've really been sweet, giving me so many gifts for Pastor's Appreciation Month," I began to tell Dave. "However, I'm a little uncomfortable because I feel these gifts have been beyond the usual measure of appreciation.

"Pastors—especially singles—have to be very careful about relationships with their parishioners, and I just want to know if something else is going on."

"Yes, there is," Dave admitted. "It started back in June. One day while I was in the hospital, I felt God told me I was going to fall in love and marry you."

If I was gaped-mouthed when Dave brought over the dozen roses, it was nothing to compare to how low my jaw hung now at this news. Dave must have read my response, because he immediately added, "My first reaction was, 'But Lord, she's a redhead!' And then I thought, 'This is not the appropriate time for such a message, God.' So I pushed the whole thing out of my mind."

Dave then told Vera about the women he had dated that summer, and how the relationships had developed. He explained to us both what happened in September when he came to the altar rail, and how God took away his pain and hurt. Dave broke off the other relationships and began to work on his relationship with God.

This is what brought him one night a couple of weeks ago to an evening service, he said. Per usual, he sat on the row right in front of where I stood to lead the Bible study. "I looked up into your eyes, and it was like God shot an arrow into my heart. For the first time since June, I remembered God's message to me about you.

"I have to tell you I still don't feel physically attracted to you," Dave added. "I've never liked redheads. I've always gone for long-legged blondes. And another thing: All the women I've ever gone with before, I felt lust for them before I felt any love. Not with you. That's why I feel this is a love from God."

"I appreciate that what you are saying is genuine," I said, noting Vera's rapt attention on the other side of the sofa. "But I have to tell you, I don't feel any attraction to you, physically or otherwise. I feel I would be unfair to you to even encourage such a relationship right now. I feel you are still vulnerable after Cathy's death, and I'd be taking advantage of a natural feeling of sympathy you would feel toward me for all I did when Cathy was sick."

Part of me wondered whether I should continue by outlining how difficult it would be for Dave to even pursue a relationship with me. After all, if he considered all the practical obstacles to a relationship, it might simply scare him away. But before I could enumerate them, he did.

"I told God I didn't want to be married to a pastor," he said. "I told God I don't want to have to pick up my business and move with you wherever you would be appointed. I told God I don't want to leave northern Michigan as my home.

"I told God all these things, but I keep getting the same answer back: That God intends for the two of us to be together, and these things will all get worked out over time. I certainly don't have all of the answers, but I do believe I have feelings for you, and I'd like to go out on a date to try and see whether they are true."

Vera couldn't help breaking her instructions, and interrupted to ask me, "If you did wish to date Dave, could you do so as pastor of Horton Bay?"

"No," I replied. "Either I would have to be moved elsewhere as a pastor, or Dave would have to leave as a member and attend another church. Besides, Dave would need to receive spiritual nourishment from another source. Anything I would say from the pulpit would be filtered through his romantic feelings for me."

Turning to Dave, I added, "I feel it would be unfair to ask you to leave Horton Bay church right now. They are a major support to you—a support another church family couldn't offer because they haven't walked through the trials with you. That's why I feel, right now, it would be impossible for us to date."

Dave admitted he didn't relish the idea of leaving Horton Bay.

"And I really must insist," I added, "no more cards or gifts. I believe you when you say your feelings are genuine, but I really feel like you need to slow down. If this is real, it will continue to be real as time passes."

Dave agreed to this, and to two more stipulations I made: That he talk to his kids and see how they felt about his feelings for me, and that he talk to another pastor to receive grief counseling. I didn't say it, but I figured either Amy or another pastor could get Dave to realize his "love" was nothing more than a special sense of gratitude.

That night, I wrote a letter back to Denny Buwalda to let him know how the meeting went. At that time, I noted, Dave had agreed to respect the boundaries I'd set forth. I believed time would resolve the feelings he believed he had for me.

At the same time, Dave wrote in his journal, *I think the Lord has touched (Kathy's) heart too, but she wouldn't and couldn't really say. She did say if anything like this was to take place, she would have to leave the church or I would. I don't think the church is ready to lose her. I'm not sure if this may be a way to move me to a different church. I don't know. I am praying and asking God to lead me and let me know what's next.*

Chapter 21

Trust in the Lord with all your heart,
and do not rely on your own insight.
—Proverbs 3:5

Shy was an adjective rarely used to describe Leslie Van De Car. Leslie had attended Horton Bay before I began serving there, but moved downstate with family shortly after I arrived. In the summer of 1998, Leslie and her husband separated, and Leslie returned to the Charlevoix area to live and to Horton Bay church to worship.

I enjoyed Leslie's company. She had a tell-it-like-it-is attitude tempered by a great sense of humor. She could tell you how rotten you were at something while she giggled, and you found yourself agreeing and laughing with her at the same time.

Leslie soon found her weekends very lonely, and suggested we start the singles group that first met in September. In early December, Leslie invited the singles to make a Christmas shopping trip to the closest shopping mall—one hour south of Horton Bay. Five persons showed up the morning of the shopping spree: Dave, Leslie, Judy Caldecott's mother Laura Kent, Doris J. Robinson (who actually was married, but wanted to go shopping) and me. Dave offered to drive us, so we jumped into his black Ford Expedition and set off for the sixty-mile trek to Traverse City.

Halfway to Traverse City, Dave casually said, "By the way, ladies, you know I'm driving you down to Traverse City for free. However, those wishing to return will be charged a kiss."

I looked sideways at Dave. The stinker. I knew what he was up to; and I figured he knew that *I* knew. But was I going to raise a fuss in front of the other women who didn't know that he knew that I knew what he knew?

Well, one lady kind of knew: Leslie. Our group had lunch at an Italian restaurant in Traverse City, and then split up at the first shopping mall. Leslie and I, who shared the same dress size, went together into a department store.

We were admiring the clothes when Leslie popped the question: "So, you sure have got Dave hooked," she said. "When are you going to reel him in?"

I think I sputtered a few minutes like a caught fish myself. "Well, it's not so easy," I began. I then laid out for her what Dave and I already had discussed: the fact that parishioners and pastors don't date; that as true as his feelings appeared to be, I didn't reciprocate, etc. Leslie was the first parishioner outside of Vera with whom I was sharing any information about Dave, so I was interested to see her response.

"I guess I hadn't considered how complicated it could be," she noted. I was pleased that she seemed to realize the ramifications outweighed any hope of a relationship between us—until an hour later, when Dave caught up with me in Sears.

"Leslie just caught me in the tool section and asked me when you were going to reel me in," Dave said.

Leslie got in one other jab that day. She and I were standing in a Christmas decoration store admiring a variety of ornaments when Dave joined us. Dave told us for Christmas, he was decorating one tree with just angels, in memory of Cathy. After he walked away, I pointed out to Leslie a particular angel I liked.

Whereupon Leslie whirled around and, in a junior-high-matchmaking-conspiracy kind of voice, called out, "Da-ave! Kathy likes this one!" Of course, Dave came back and bought it.

As much as I wanted to kick Leslie at the moment, I was more preoccupied with Dave's comment about a kiss. To offer a kiss of appreciation seemed innocent enough, particularly given the holiday season and feelings. However, my gut feeling was Dave would misinterpret it. At the same time, to refuse—especially if all the other ladies complied—would call more attention to the situation than I desired.

Our last stop was Meijer's Thrifty Acre, where all of us went our own ways. We agreed to meet at the front of the store in one hour. About ten minutes before the deadline, I stood up front mulling over the dilemma as Doris and Laura joined me.

Then, I felt God nudge me with a wonderful bit of whimsical wisdom. With a grin, I said to the ladies, "Remember how Dave said each of us owed him a kiss for the trip home? Wouldn't it be funny if each of us were to give him a Hershey's Kiss?"

Doris loved the idea, and headed back into the candy section. She emerged with a handful of Hershey's Kisses and Dove Promises. "This way, we can give him a Kiss *and* a Promise!" she said, as she brought her purchases back up front.

Fortunately, Leslie joined us before Dave finished his shopping. Doris passed out the chocolates, which we quickly tucked away in our coat pockets as Dave approached.

Dave led us out of the store and through the parking lot back to the Expedition. "So, ladies," he said, in that same casual tone of voice, "where are my kisses?"

And one by one, we walked up, dropped a Kiss and Promise into Dave's hand, and climbed into the vehicle.

Dave knew he'd been had. And he knew that *I* knew, this little plan of his had just been completely undermined. But he took it in good stride, and climbed into the driver's seat for the ride home, laughing with the rest of us.

His day did not end completely kiss-free. After we arrived home in the church parking lot, Laura Kent gave Dave a peck on the cheek. A kiss from the seventy-plus-year-old was not what Dave had in mind that day, but aside from a chocolate buzz, it was the most he got that day.

Chapter

By faith, Abraham obeyed when he was called to set out for a place that he was to receive as an inheritance; and he set out, not knowing where he was going.
—Hebrews 11:8

The old school at Horton Bay United Methodist Church insisted on specific Christmas tree decorations. Aside from the tinsel, the only decorations allowed were Chrismons—decorations with specific Christian symbolism.

No one protested in 1998, however, when Dave added an ornament of his own: a miniature drum with Cathy's picture on the front side.

About two weeks before Christmas, Dave came to see me. "How do I go about leaving the church?" he asked.

I looked at him a little befuddled. "What do you mean 'leave'? Do you mean simply attending another church, or removing your membership from the rolls?"

"I mean removing my membership," Dave said. "I have tried to put some distance between me and you, and yet it seems like we naturally keep ending up together. The feelings I have for you aren't going away, and I feel like God is telling me I need to leave the church."

"Are you sure this is what you want to do?" I asked. "I hate the thought of you not having Horton Bay's people to support you, especially at Christmas time. I don't like the idea that you'd be leaving the church so you can date me."

"This isn't about you," Dave replied, a little astonished. "If I left the church, we may or may not date—I don't know. I just know God is telling me to go someplace else, and I feel like I need to obey, even if I don't know why."

"I'll tell you what," I said. "Consider what you'd be doing for another week. If you still believe this is what God wants, write me a letter, requesting that your name be removed from our membership books."

One week before Christmas, Dave returned to the parsonage. This time, he had a letter with his formal request to be removed as a member.

I flipped to the "C" page in the membership book, and marked a "W" by Dave's name for withdrawn. My eyes couldn't help going to the name below his: Cathy Cadarette, also marked with a "W."

During this same time, Dave submitted to two of my requests: he met with another pastor for counseling, and he talked to his kids about his feelings for me. He told me the pastor said Dave seemed to have made up his mind; the boys said they just wanted him to be happy; and Amy told him he should go slowly. I always thought Amy was the smartest Cadarette.

However, Dave broke one of his promises to me: the no-gift policy. First, he showed up at my door with roses: thirty-nine roses, to be exact. I'd seen fewer roses on display at some florists' shops. But there they were: thirty-eight red ones, each marking a year of my life, and one white one to show his thankfulness to Jesus.

"You promised no presents," I protested.

Dave just flashed me that Cadarette grin.

A couple of days later, Dave showed up with four wrapped presents. Knowing I collected Noah's arks, Dave had gotten me a cloth ark with stuffed animals and a Noah's ark ornament. He also got me two coffee cups. One was thimble sized with my name inscribed on it. The other had Noah and the animals, and words from Ecclesiastes: "Two are better than one."

"What is this, propaganda?" I asked Dave.

"What's propaganda," he replied.

"Never mind," I said, adding the presents to others given to me by parishioners.

At the midweek service before Christmas, Dave finally shared with those attending about his summer affairs, his renewal with

God, his subsequent feelings for me, and his plans to leave the church and attend another in the community.

"Can't he just go to Greensky Hill?" one member asked when Dave finished.

"No, because Dave needs someone other than me to be his pastor right now," I explained. "I accept that Dave's feelings are genuine, but right now, I can't say that I feel anything for him. For him to continue to worship here would be difficult for him and for me."

Most members didn't want Dave to leave, and tried to persuade me to talk him out of it. I reminded them how God tested Abraham. After Abraham demonstrated his faith by leaving his home, God had asked what sounded impossible: God asked Abraham to offer his only son, Isaac, as a sacrifice.

Maybe this is why Abraham didn't tell anyone else what God had asked, I told parishioners. Abraham knew how crazy it sounded, and knew people would try to talk him out of it. Yet he also knew beyond any doubt that the command was from God, and his only response could be one of obedience.

As word spread in our congregation, Dave decided to share the news with Jan Leist, Cathy's best friend. When he told me he was going to talk to her, I secretly applauded. If anyone could assure Dave that he needed to slow down and rethink everything, Jan would.

Within an hour, Dave knocked on the front door. I put on my best "I know you didn't want to hear this, but it was for your own good" face as we sat across from each other at the kitchen table.

"Well," Dave said, taking a deep breath, "I started to tell her everything—about last summer, about how God took away that empty feeling in my heart. Then I started to tell her that there was someone new in my life, and she said, 'Stop right there.'"

Way to go, Jan, I thought inwardly. But then Dave continued:

"Jan told me that three years ago, when Cathy was undergoing one of the harsh chemo treatments, Jan stopped to visit her in the hospital. Seeing how sick Cathy was, and knowing how serious the cancer was, Jan left the hospital in tears."

Jan continued on her route as a mail carrier, but was crying and praying the whole distance. "What is going to happen to Dave," she asked God in the midst of her tears.

And suddenly, Jan told Dave, she felt God present with her. Jan said God told her Dave would fall in love again and remarry, and while the new woman also would be called Cathy, she would be one whose name started with a K.

I sat stunned for a second. When I finally met Dave's eyes again, he was wearing that "I know you didn't want to hear this, but it was for your own good" face.

As Christmas Eve approached, Dave called. "Come to dinner at my house before the Christmas Eve service," he said. "It will be family, the Koteskeys and Vera Hallman."

I tried protesting, but Dave wouldn't accept any answer other than "OK." At the appointed time, I arrived at Dave's house with Vera. When we walked in, Dave stood grinning at the end of the hallway. I was a little surprised he didn't come to greet us, so I started toward him.

As soon as I reached him, Dave's eyes went from my eyes up above his head and then down again. I looked up: there was a sprig of mistletoe.

Dave says my reaction was like that of cartoon characters whose eyes go wide open with a loud "Boing!" I didn't hear a "boing," but I know my eyes were wide as I looked back at Dave.

"Don't worry, I won't insist on a kiss," Dave said grinning, and moved back toward the kitchen. Thank goodness, I thought—I'd left all my Hershey's Kisses at home!

That night, we concluded the Horton Bay service singing *Silent Night*, lighting candles held by persons in the pews. For some parishioners, the service had a sense of loss, as it was the first Christmas Eve since Cathy died, and they knew Dave would be absent from his pew the following Sunday. For Dave, however, there was a sense of perfect peace.

Dave had offered to drive me that night to Traverse City where I was catching my flight to Indianapolis. I had a lot of reasons to accept, as the roads were snowy and Dave had four-wheel drive.

However, I felt I needed to show Dave I was an independent lady. (Actually, he would call it stubborn, and we both would be right!) I'd reluctantly accepted the gifts and the Christmas Eve dinner. What I needed was to see Dave accept a few of my decisions and allow me to stick by my guns when I felt I was right—and know

Dave wasn't trying to use me as a substitute for his feelings of grief for Cathy that holiday season.

On Christmas night, Dave wrote, *Happy birthday, Jesus. Had a pretty good day today. I thought this would be a hard day, being it's the first Christmas without Mom. It was nice to go down and wish her a merry Christmas at the bridge, but I knew she wasn't there. But we all took the time together to pray, and she was there. Brent's poem was good. The cry was nice and I'm so thankful Mom is feeling fine and not sick and she still gets to be with us all of the time.*

I wish it didn't take me so long to know what the Lord's trying to teach me. I hope this doesn't make Mom feel bad when it does. Jesus probably shows her the end result ahead of time.

Chapter

He said, "Abba, Father, for you all things are possible; remove this cup from me; yet, not what I want, but what you want."

—Mark 14: 36

Considering how he felt at the time, I'm surprised Dave didn't record January 2, 1999 in his journal. On the other hand, he's told the story so many times, he doesn't need a written record to remember the details.

Dave had called me shortly after I arrived home from Indiana. "January 2 is my birthday," he said. "I get free ski passes from Boyne Highlands because of the work I do there. How about coming cross-country skiing with me for my birthday?"

I wasn't a great cross-country skier, but I enjoyed it enough to invest in my own skis, boots and poles. Usually, Judy Caldecott and I would head to Young State Park for our favorite winter wonderland.

I agreed to go with Dave on Saturday, and could hear the delight in his voice.

As the weekend approached, Amy called her dad from Grand Rapids. "Would you like me to come up this weekend for your birthday, so you won't be alone?" she asked.

"No, I have plans with P.K.," he told her. "We're going skiing together."

But on Friday, New Year's Day, I was beginning to get cold feet at the thought of skiing with Dave. Not only was I getting nervous at the idea of being alone with him, I wondered how he'd respond if I wasn't as accomplished a skier as he was. I didn't know what would be worse: Dave getting amorous, or my being stuck in a snowdrift while he laughed at me.

I put the teakettle on the stove and went to the living room to curl up for thought. Was I ready for a relationship with any man, let alone Dave Cadarette?

After all, I'd been single for thirty-eight years of my life, and I'd gotten pretty good at it. I had prayed more than a couple of times to God that if I were to be single all my life, that would be fine; however, if there were to be a Mr. Right in my life, I'd sure appreciate some notice!

The only man I ever considered marrying was my dad. Of course, I was six years old at the time. But there's a lot of truth in the notion that girls marry men who remind them of their fathers. Because of my father, I had most definite ideas about the type of man I would marry.

First of all, he would be a Christian. The foundation of our home would have to be Christ, and no other. Seeing my Dad say grace, read his Bible and lead worship services at Eden brought greater meaning because it was in tandem with Mom's spirituality.

Second, my husband had to have a sense of humor. All of the Slaughters loved to laugh, but especially my dad. When he laughed, Dad's whole being was enveloped in joy. His smile would sneak up beyond his mouth until it reached his blue eyes, and his shoulders would shake with each chuckle.

I also wanted to be sure I married someone who would be as committed to the marriage as me. My parents had their share of rocky places in their life together, but they vowed to work them out together. I didn't want anyone who thought divorce was an option for "working out" any differences of opinions.

Finally, my husband would have to be kind. I realize most people would believe that to be part and parcel of being Christian. However, my dad had learned a special kindness from his parents— a kindness that didn't require others to ask for help, but simply filled the need as best he was able.

As the teakettle whistle drew my thoughts back to the present, I returned to the kitchen. Dumping a teabag and one and a half teaspoons of sugar into my cup, I added the hot water and watched the sugar dissolve. As it did so, I suddenly realized with a start: Dave was a Christian. Dave was funny. Dave was committed. And just last week, as I watched Dave escort Vera Hallman up her steps, and then take five minutes to shovel the snow off her porch, steps and front sidewalk, I'd been reminded of my dad's kindness.

I picked up my hot tea and returned to the living room. My tortoise shell cat, Meesha, strolled into the living room and stopped in front of the sofa. She purred for a few seconds until she realized the aroma from the teacup had nothing to do with tuna. Losing interest, she began to give herself a bath, but I took little notice as my thoughts raced.

Everyone kept asking me, "How do you feel about Dave?" I'd said things like he was a good man, he was handsome, but he wasn't my type.

But the question now kept hitting me, as if we'd reached that moment when Jesus turned to His disciples and asked, "Who do you say that I am?" How did I feel about Dave?

When it came to Dave and me, I knew how the church felt; I knew how Dave's kids felt; I knew how Jan felt; I knew how my parents felt.

I even, although I was trying to deny it, believed I knew how God felt. Dave said he had received a message in the hospital from God that we would marry, although Dave's first reaction had been, "But Lord, she's a redhead!"

What I was withholding from everyone was the fact that while I had been in the hospital, I too felt God had told me, "One day, you will marry Dave." And my first reaction had been, "But Lord, he's a hockey player!"

But like Dave, my second response was, "This is not the time nor place for such a message. If it is from God, I will hear it again. But not now."

So in all that Dave had told me, I'd been keeping hidden what God had told me. But even deeper, I was keeping hidden the essential question: How did I, Kathy Slaughter, feel about David Cadarette Sr.?

And in that moment, I realized I didn't want to open that door: I didn't want to know or at least admit how I felt about Dave. I felt like this door separated me from my feelings and if I tried to peek behind it, the door would be flung open, never to be closed again.

What was I afraid of, I thought, as I continued to sip my tea. Yes, Dave and I were opposites, but other opposites had successful marriages. Case in point: my mother had been salutatorian of her high school class; my father wrote letters to her addressed "to my sweatheart."

Was I afraid of trying to fill Cathy's place in Dave's life? After all, whoever married Dave would always be the second wife. She'd always be the stepmother and step grandmother, etc. At holidays and celebrations, people would naturally talk of Cathy and how they missed her—even as the new Mrs. Cadarette sat by.

As Meesha finished her bath, I called her until she jumped up into my lap and curled into a ball. As I stroked her, I remembered my counseling appointment with Dave that August. I had warned Dave of the danger of trying to use a new relationship as a means to escape his grief.

There's my fear, I realized: I felt Dave wanted me there on this first birthday without Cathy as a way to smother any memories or feelings he had of Cathy. And my initial acceptance of his invitation wasn't because I loved being with him or even loved him—it was out of a sense of obligation to Dave, and even to Cathy, that he wouldn't be alone that day.

I would be able to go skiing with Dave with a completely clear conscience if I believed both of us were there because we felt love for each other. But, I realized in that moment, it wasn't the case. I felt pity for Dave, and that was a sorry foundation for any relationship—even if God were the one bringing us together.

"Lord," I prayed, "I don't know what you have in mind for Dave and me. But until I have a clear sign from you that it's OK for me to admit and accept how I feel about Dave, I'm not ready to pursue any relationship with him."

Heading back into the kitchen, I put my teacup in the sink, and then picked up the phone and dialed a number I knew by heart. "Hey, it's me," I said as Dave answered. "I'm sorry, but I just remembered—I already said I'd go to Jody Piper's surprise birthday party tomorrow. I completely forgot about it. I can't go skiing with you."

Over the phone, Dave sounded his usual easy going self and said we'd go another time. (Of course, every time he's told the story since then, he's added words like "crushed" and "devastated.")

For a few days, I felt bad that indeed I might have hurt Dave; on the other hand, if the timing wasn't God's, I wasn't going to push it. If God intended for us to be together, I needed a clear sign that this was His will.

As Dave and I were about to learn, God's timing was about to come.

Chapter 24

But Ruth said, "Do not press me to leave you or to turn back from following you! Where you go, I will go; where you lodge, I will lodge; your people shall be my people, and your God, my God."
—Ruth 1:16

Unfortunately, the hot tea didn't stop my least favorite holiday tradition: the post-holiday letdown that leads to me getting a cold or flu.

One week after I broke my date with Dave, I was directing a wedding rehearsal at Greensky Hill when I began to feel pain. I'd never had a bladder infection, but the symptoms made me suspect I was getting my first one.

With the old "show must go on" attitude, I didn't say anything to the couple and conducted their wedding without any problems Saturday. As soon as it was finished, however, I knew I needed to get to a doctor.

I drove from the church to Petoskey to a walk-in clinic; unfortunately, it was closed. I drove home and, within a few minutes, Dave called. "How is everything?" he asked.

"Oh, fine," I said, grimacing as I eased myself onto the sofa. I knew if I asked him to take me to the doctor, he'd be there in seconds. However, I just couldn't. We chatted for a few minutes, and—as soon as he hung up—I called Jeannie Babbitt and asked if she'd take me to the Charlevoix Hospital emergency room.

Sure enough, the doctor's diagnosis was bladder infection, and he started me on antibiotics. Jeannie drove me to a drugstore to get the medication, then took me home.

While Dave was unaware of what was happening with me that night, I was unaware of something he was doing. For on January 9, as he prepared for bed, Dave prayed, "Father, I give up. I can't change Kathy's mind about the love you have given to me for her. If this is your will, you'll have to convince her. You'll have to be the one to persuade her that this is your will."

The next morning, Dave came to Horton Bay after attending worship at Petoskey United Methodist Church. He walked in during the children's message and joined a group of us for lunch afterwards. But he said nothing to me that day about his prayer.

That night, between the infection and still performing all my duties as pastor, I was whipped. I gratefully went to bed early and fell asleep immediately.

However, in the middle of the night, I suddenly awoke. I glanced at the clock to see it was 1:14. I quickly closed my eyes, debating for what seemed like just seconds whether to make a trip to the bathroom or to try to fall back asleep as fast as possible. When I opened my eyes again, the clock read 1:17.

The next day, Jan Leist's family used the Education Wing at Horton Bay for a dinner following the funeral of a relative. Unfortunately, the infection and medication were making me dizzy and sick, so I called to let the church officers know I wouldn't be there.

As the ladies were cleaning up, one of them fixed two plates of food for me. Dave offered to take them to me, and walked across the parking lot with a plate in each hand.

I'm still surprised he didn't drop both of them when I opened the door. My face was flushed with fever; my eyes were half open and dull. I'd been napping on a couch, so my hair was flat on one side and sticking out on the other. I hadn't even brushed my teeth, so morning breath had become afternoon breath.

Without missing a beat, Dave said, "You look awful."

Well, at least love isn't blind, I thought. Count on Dave for giving me his honest opinion.

Assured that I wasn't hungry then, but I would eat later, Dave put the food in the refrigerator. "Can I pray for you?" he asked, and then putting his hands on my shoulders, he prayed for God's healing power to work in me.

I hit the bed early although, with all of my naps, it was harder to sleep. Soon, I opened my eyes and saw that it was 1:14. I went to the bathroom and came back to bed to find the clock now read 1:17.

Funny, those were the exact same times I saw last night, I thought as I lay down again.

Tuesday, I was back on track physically. I went to bed at my usual time and went right to sleep. But promptly at 1:14, I awoke to see the time. I closed my eyes, determined to go back to sleep. But when I glanced at the clock again, it was 1:17.

OK, now God had my attention. Surely God was giving me that sign. I had told Cathy it was OK to ask God for a sign, and I had essentially asked Him for one regarding Dave. However, I wished God would be a little clearer.

I tried to think of the significance of the numbers, and considered maybe something would happen between the dates of 1/14—which was Wednesday—and 1/17.

I asked Dave whether the numbers 1:14 or 1:17 had any meaning. "No, why?" he said.

"I keep seeing those numbers on my clock alarm every night for the past three nights," I said. "I can't put any meaning to them, and thought maybe the dates were significant to you."

Dave confessed he was as puzzled as me, but neither of us gave it any more thought.

That is, until 1:14 A.M. Thursday when I again was awakened from a dead sleep. "What can you mean?" I prayed to God. "What is it you're trying to tell me?"

And then I exclaimed, "Dummy (meaning me, not God!)! The reference must be to scripture: chapter 1, verses 14-17!"

No sooner had the thought crossed my mind, than I felt the Holy Spirit whisper to me: "Look at Ruth 1:14-17. This is your sign."

I immediately grabbed a Bible from my office, went into the living room, and opened the Bible—to Genesis. "It's not that I don't trust you," I explained aloud to God. "It's just that I don't trust me. I'm going to check all of the other books of the Bible first. If anything else speaks to me, then this is all coincidence. It's not a sign from you; it's just weird insomnia!"

So I checked through all the other sixty-five books, skipping over Ruth. I found nothing—not a single portion of scripture spoke to me.

Then, holding my breath, I turned the pages back to Ruth. In its opening chapter, the Israelite Naomi plans to return to her homeland after her husband and sons died in the land of Moab. Her two daughters-in-law—Orpah and Ruth—plan to travel to Israel with Naomi, but she urges them to return to Moab, the land of their birth and their family.

And then these words in Ruth 1:14-17:

> Then they wept aloud again. Orpah kissed her mother-in-law, but Ruth clung to her.
> So [Naomi] said, "See, your sister-in-law has gone back to her people and to her gods; return after your sister-in-law." But Ruth said,
> "Do not press me to leave you or to turn back from following you!
> Where you go, I will go; where you lodge, I will lodge;
> Your people shall be my people, and your God my God.
> Where you die, I will die—there will I be buried.
> May the Lord do thus and so to me and more as well,
> If even death parts me from you."

As I read these words, the tears began flowing as I again felt the Holy Spirit present with me in that room. "You've been a good Naomi," I felt God saying to me. "You recognize your differences from Dave, you have raised all the right questions, and made all the right arguments as to why Dave and you should be apart.

"But I want you to know Dave's love is as sincere as Ruth's, and just as stubborn. You can trust Dave. The two of you could be one. Your people could be his people, and I could be his God. But the decision is yours."

And as I wept, I finally understood. God had brought me to Horton Bay to prepare me for Dave. I got the chance to meet, to know, to love and to mourn for his Cathy. Even as a stepmother and step grandmother, I would feel pride knowing in whose steps I followed. In the family memories of Cathy, I would feel no threat.

Rather, I too would feel joy and love at being a part of this special woman's life.

In turn, I also realized God had been preparing Dave for me. God had taken this man of passion and impulse and, through the past six months, had taught him self-control and patience—virtues he would need as the husband of a pastor.

But I also knew one more thing. God needed me to now say yes. Even with all the plans and best intentions God had for me, God gave me a free will. Just as God had called me to be a pastor, but needed my acceptance and submission to His will, in this moment I could accept or reject His plans for a life married to Dave.

So in my tears, I accepted. "I confess to you that I am afraid of the unknown," I said. "I confess that I've been a very independent person for thirty-eight years, and I'm going to need all of your wisdom and strength to be a wife.

"But I give control to you in my life. If we are to be man and wife, let it be so."

And finally, that door I'd been holding closed on my feelings opened. I remembered, just after Cathy's funeral, how I had called the Cadarette home and heard Dave's new message on the answering machine. Instead of the usual spark, Dave's voice was wracked with grief. I wanted to reach out and hug him as I heard the pain in his voice.

I thought of the previous Sunday when he walked into the sanctuary, how my face lit up and my hand automatically lifted to greet him.

And for the first time, I thought: I, Kathy Slaughter, love David Cadarette.

Still, when Dave called Friday, I became shy. Instead of directly telling him what I thought the verses meant, I told him he should read Ruth 1:14-17. We agreed to meet for lunch Saturday with our friend, Vera.

As Dave drove the three of us home, Dave casually asked me, "Would you like to go to watch me play hockey tonight?"

To his and Vera's surprise, I said, "Yes."

So it was that on a Saturday night, Dave and I were alone together, riding up to Cheboygan. At the ice rink, I sat alone, watching Dave playing hockey. Since I was completely ignorant of the rules of the game, I was grateful Brent was on the opposing team. At least that way, I could applaud regardless of what either team did!

On the way home, Dave and I talked nonstop about everything—I shared with him my vision, and what I felt God was saying. He shared with me that the previous Saturday night, he had finally given up control to God—which explained why God's sign came when it did.

When we arrived home at the parsonage, Dave and I hugged. We didn't kiss that night. We didn't need to. There was something much more important we needed to do.

Because Dave could finally say the three words he'd longed to say, but knew he couldn't until the time was right. For now as we hugged, he said, "I love you."

And I was finally able to say the words I wanted to say back: "I love you, too."

Chapter 25

*We know that all things work together for good
for those who love God, who are called
according to his purpose.*
—Romans 8:28

May 22, 1999 didn't dawn as the wedding day most brides want. The clouds were thick and hinted at rain, although the forecast was for a sunny afternoon.

As the bride, however, I didn't mind. With more than two hundred people planning to attend Dave's and my wedding that morning, a cloudy sky meant a cooler church.

Events had come quickly between our first date and that wedding date. On January 17, Dave accompanied me to services at both Greensky and Horton Bay churches, where we announced the sign I had received from God, and that we would appreciate the congregation's prayers for us. That night, I shared this in a phone call to my parents who were wintering in Tucson, Arizona.

The next day, I accompanied Dave to Flint where he was picking his parents up at the airport. We both realized as we traveled that our conversation was not idle chitchat. Those who later were surprised by the quickness of our engagement weren't aware of the depth of our conversations in those first few days. Instead of small talk about the weather and such, we seriously discussed our thoughts on future children, careers and families.

Even I wasn't prepared, however, that Monday—two days after our first date—when Dave suddenly asked, "So, will you marry me?"

"Probably," I replied. That wasn't the answer Dave wanted, but he did get his first kiss that day, after we said grace for our meal in the parking lot at McDonald's in Bay City.

That night, I called my parents again. "Now, I want to be clear about my relationship with Dave," I said. "We were talking about the 'M' word today, and there may be a wedding before the end of the year."

The next night, another full day of discussions with Dave, I called my parents and asked, "So, how does May 22 sound to you?"

At the end of our third call in as many nights, my mom said, "By the way, honey, don't call tomorrow night unless it's an emergency. Your dad and I are beginning to think that you and Dave have already eloped, and this is just your way of breaking it to us gently!"

On Friday, Dave and I went to the jewelry store. Because our rings needed to be resized, we walked out of the store empty-handed. The next morning, Dave came to the parsonage and slipped a white bread-bag twisty-tie around my finger. "Until the real one comes in," he said.

We'd wanted to hold off announcing our formal engagement until Valentine's Day. However, we told Vera Hallman with instructions not to tell anyone. But she told one person, who told another, who told another—and by Saturday, all of Charlevoix knew. We made it official Sunday, as I announced our engagement at Greensky and Dave did so at Horton Bay.

The pulpit had become a familiar place for Dave, who had stood there to announce his feelings for me, his decision to leave the congregation and, just the week before, of our decision to date. As he came to the pulpit in Horton Bay that morning, he said, "How many people are nervous seeing me up here again?"

He was tickled when a number of people laughed. What he didn't know was, behind him, I had raised my hand.

As our wedding date approached, our physical passion began to increase. When ordained as a pastor, I took a vow of celibacy as a single person—an easy vow to keep while I was single and not dating. However, Dave and I both vowed we would hold off physical intimacy until our wedding night, and we did.

We'd considered having a summer or September wedding. However, I knew how busy my schedule was in the summer, and knew Dave's was just as full with roofing jobs. Rather than trying to plan a wedding at the height of our busiest time of the year, we decided on May 22.

That morning, I awoke early. My dress was hanging on the back of the bedroom door. I checked the weather report, and then greeted my parents and sister as they arrived from the motel. Jody Piper soon arrived to work on my hair, and then my mom's.

I was working on my makeup an hour before the service when the phone rang. I heard someone get it, and then they called out, "It's Dave. He wants you to know you've got an hour to change your mind."

Dave was supposed to be at the church forty-five minutes before the service. When Amy arrived at the parsonage, she said somewhat in disgust, "Dad's still soaking in the bathtub."

But with fifteen minutes to spare, Dave arrived and went into the church. He stood and made small talk with Pastor Dave Morton, my mentor from Battle Creek who was performing the wedding. Best man Dick Rickard walked over to join him, along with groomsmen Brent and David Jr. They soon walked to the front of the sanctuary.

At the parsonage, I was getting final approval on my appearance by my matron of honor, Shirley Ross, and bridesmaids Amy and my sister-in-law, Jennifer. Each of them carried an ivory rose; I carried the same Bible my mother had carried when she married Dad.

As we started to walk from the parsonage to the church, I found the parking lot packed with cars. I soon learned every seat was taken in the pews and the numerous folding chairs we'd set up in the Education Wing. However, everyone had a seat as the service began.

As we stood in the back of the church, we heard Barb Borgeld sing *Here I Am, Lord*—Cathy's favorite hymn. At their cue, my bridesmaids disappeared through the swinging doors of the bell tower, taking their places at the front of the sanctuary with the men. As the first notes of *Here Comes the Bride* began, I squeezed Dad's arm and we started forward.

At first, I couldn't see Dave because all the people were standing. As soon as we turned the corner of the aisle, however, I saw him. At that moment, he was looking down. For that moment, I think we both had the same thought. For all the joy we were feeling—for all the love and laughter that would follow our union—we'd have traded it all if Cathy could have been alive, and she and Dave were still husband and wife.

However, when Dave looked up and our eyes met, each of us broke into huge smiles as we realized the good God had worked through our circumstances—a very present help, bringing us together in this place of friends and family in honor of God.

The service was traditional, including the father giving away his daughter. (Dad worried that he'd forget his line, so we had a computer banner with "Her mother and I" hanging on our side of the railing!) However, as Pastor Dave invited us to exchange our vows, Dave and I read the words we had written ourselves for this special day:

> *I, David, take you Kathryn, to be my wife*
> *I, Kathryn, take you, David, to be my husband,*
> *Never ask me to leave you, or not to follow you.*
> *Where you go, I will go. Where you live I will live.*
> *Your people will be my people, and Your God will be my God.*
> *May God help us to keep our vows for as long as we both*
> *shall live.*

A Very Present Help
Order Form

Postal orders: 05925 Horton Bay Rd.
Boyne City, MI 49712

Telephone orders: (231) 582-6906

E-mail orders: davec@racc2000.com

Please send *A Very Present Help* to:

Name: _____

Address: _____

City: _____   State: _____

Zip: _____

Telephone: (_____) _____

Book Price: $12.00

Shipping: $3.00 for the first book and $1.00 for each additional book to
cover shipping and handling within US, Canada, and Mexico.
International orders add $6.00 for the first book and $2.00 for
each additional book.

Or order from:
ACW Press
85334 Lorane Hwy
Eugene, OR 97405

(800) 931-BOOK

or contact your local bookstore